Releasing
the Knot
of the Mind

Releasing the Knot of the Mind

Instructions on Resting
in Stillness and Awareness

*A commentary on Dudjom Lingpa's
Dzogchen meditation guide*

ANAM THUBTEN

WITH A FOREWORD BY
DUNGSE JIGME WANGDRAK RINPOCHE

SHAMBHALA

Shambhala Publications, Inc.
2129 13th Street
Boulder, Colorado 80302
www.shambhala.com

© 2026 by Anam Thubten

Cover art: "Namkha Drime" by Lhaksam Kunkyut
Cover design: Daniel Urban-Brown and Meredith Jarrett
Interior design: Meredith Jarrett

All rights reserved. No part of this book may be reproduced in any form or by any means, electronic or mechanical, including photocopying, recording, or by any information storage and retrieval system, without permission in writing from the publisher.

9 8 7 6 5 4 3 2 1

First Edition
Printed in the United States of America

Shambhala Publications makes every effort to print on acid-free, recycled paper. Shambhala Publications is distributed worldwide by Penguin Random House, Inc., and its subsidiaries.

Library of Congress Cataloging-in-Publication Data
Names: Thubten, Anam, author. | Jigme Wangdrak, Chakung, other.
Title: Releasing the knot of the mind: Instructions on resting in stillness and awareness / Anam Thubten; with a foreword by Jigme Wangdrak Rinpoche.
Description: First edition. | Boulder: Shambhala Publications, 2026. |
Identifiers: LCCN 2025036641 | ISBN 9781645475446 trade paperback
Subjects: LCSH: Rdzogs-chen | Meditation—Buddhism | Rnying-ma-pa (Sect)—Doctrines
Classification: LCC BQ7662.4 .T48 2026 | DDC 294.3/444—dc23/eng
/20250923
LC record available at https://lccn.loc.gov/2025036641

The authorized representative in the EU for product safety and compliance is eucomply OÜ, Pärnu mnt 139b-14, 11317 Tallinn, Estonia, hello@eucompliancepartner.com.

Contents

Foreword by Dungse Jigme Wangdrak Rinpoche vii

Preface ix

Note on Language Conventions xiii

Song of Realization 1

Invoking the Blessings of the Lineage 7

    1. Dzogchen Master Dudjom Lingpa 9

    2. Devotion: The Path to Freedom 17

The Art of Stillness 23

    3. Understanding the Mind 25

    4. The Practice of Shamatha 37

    5. Shamatha Experiences 49

Abiding in Open Awareness 59

    6. Doorways to Awareness 61

    7. Dzogchen Inquiry 83

Contents

8. Meditation Guidance   95

Navigating the Inner Journey   105

9. The Dance of the Inner Maras   107
10. Overcoming Hindrances   131

The Art of Living in Awareness   141

11. Maintaining Awareness   143
12. Engaging with Life   157

May It Be Auspicious   177

13. Kyor Jung: Reviewing the Teachings   179
14. The Wish-Fulfilling Gem of Dzogchen   189

Appendix: Guided Meditation   195

About the Author   201

Foreword

I pay homage to the supreme refuge gurus, the regents of the Primordial Buddha.

The writings of many indisputably qualified great *tertons* state that the great terton Trakthung Dudjom Lingpa was the emanation of Guru Dorje Drolo in human form. This fact is even more illuminated when you read his writings: *Secret Experiential Autobiography* and *Questions and Answers with the Wisdom Dakinis*.

Furthermore, whether such a master is authentic or not is primarily judged based on the authenticity of his or her teachings. All the profound revelations, pith instructions of Dzogchen, and oral instructions of profound view and doctrine, which spring from the expanse of his enlightened mind, are undoubtedly blazing with the power of blessings and present us with the opportunity for swift realization. Many of Dudjom Lingpa's followers and disciples were awakened and are awakening in the realm of the great rainbow body from practicing his teachings.

I have delightful news to share: Anam Thubten Rinpoche just completed a commentary titled *Releasing the Knot of the Mind* on an inspiring oral instruction from Dudjom Lingpa. This text is

Foreword

concise, profound in meaning, endowed with the vital points of view and meditation, appropriate for today's time, and is certain to be a medicine for the mind.

I am sincerely grateful to Anam Thubten Rinpoche for writing this book and sincerely congratulate him on its publication, which is a precious spiritual gift, beneficial not only for Tibetan Buddhists but for people from all walks of life in the East and West.

This was written and offered by Chakung Jigme Wangdrak from the vicinity of the mountain of Margyal Bomra, on July 11, 2025.

DUNGSE JIGME WANGDRAK RINPOCHE

Preface

Many cultures around the world are rapidly changing due to modernization, technology, and the easy flow of information. This also comes with huge changes in our way of life, our thinking, and even our consciousness. In many ways, people are becoming more secular. The changes we are witnessing are not inherently bad; there is a litany of good things to say about them.

At the same time, some of us feel grief seeing ancient sacred traditions dissolve and play less of a role in the lives of many. These ancient traditions have so much profound wisdom, as well as disciplines and meditative methods, that can help us find inner peace and a healthy way of working with our internal turmoil. They can even lead us to transcendent inner freedom.

I feel that grief on a personal level and have the aspiration to be a small force in sustaining the ancient yet timeless wisdom of Tibetan Buddhism. In some ways, this is also my job as a Buddhist teacher. Therefore, I often try to interpret the teachings of the extraordinary masters of the past in more accessible language. One of the things I truly love to do is write contemporary commentaries on ancient spiritual texts. My intention behind this is

Preface

to create a bridge between people in the modern world and these priceless teachings.

I grew up in Eastern Tibet and trained in Tibetan Buddhism, but I have been traveling to places where Tibetan Buddhism is either new or not so well known. In those places, I usually teach the wisdom of ancient Tibetan Buddhist masters, especially those of the Nyingma lineage, using contemporary language.

Among the masters of the Nyingma lineage, Dudjom Lingpa is my North Star, and his teachings have been a bright light in my life. Coming across his teachings in this life is like finding a *chintamani*, a "wish-fulfilling gem." Not only do I try to apply his teachings in my life, I also share them with others everywhere I travel and teach.

Recently, Dungse Jigme Wangdrak Rinpoche, the fourth descendant of Dudjom Lingpa, asked me to write a commentary on a *doha*, or "song of realization," by Dudjom Lingpa. Rinpoche, a man of great discernment, does not lightly ask someone to write a commentary on Dudjom Lingpa's work. I joyously accepted his request, feeling that the process of writing this book would bring me even closer to the unfathomable mind of Dudjom Lingpa.

And yet, his request and my joyous acceptance are not totally accidental. There are many auspicious connections between me and Dudjom Lingpa, some of which are beyond the scope of our logical thinking mind. I feel my karmic connection to Dudjom Lingpa is very deep and ancient, one that has been the ground for my spiritual journey. Every time I experience that connection, I feel I am put back on the right track.

Many people today are interested in spiritual practices, meditation, and understanding consciousness and the mind. Buddhist

Preface

meditation is embraced these days by countless people, transcending culture, religion, and languages. The impact of Buddhist meditation is apparent in the lives of many people who practice it, and its benefits have been proven in modern times through a series of scientific studies. It helps people work with internal issues, such as anxiety due to fear and trauma, and cultivate the ability to be in the present moment.

However, sometimes meditation can be so simplified that it may miss the important elements of transcendence, enlightenment, and universal love. My hope is that writing a commentary on this profound doha will help anyone understand the depth of Dzogchen meditation, regardless of who they are, and help them find the means to taste true inner liberation.

Spirit Rock Meditation Center in Northern California is physically enchanting and is a land blessed by many spiritual teachers and the thousands of meditators who practiced there. When Spirit Rock invited me to co-teach a meditation retreat, I thought, "This is such an auspicious circumstance to begin the commentary." I took the initiative to follow that thought, and the moment I began to write, I felt huge waves of joy permeate my heart. The book was begun on the summer solstice of 2024 and completed a year later on the summer solstice of 2025.

I am thankful to my good friend and editor, Laura Duggan, who generously offered her time and talent to edit this book. I'm thankful to all my friends on this journey who constantly inspire and support me. If not for them, I might not have found the right conditions to create this book.

Through the merit of writing this book, may I always be in the mandala of Dudjom Lingpa, for this lifetime and beyond.

Preface

My aspiration for those who come across this book is that they will fall in love with Dudjom Lingpa's work. Through that love, may they see their true nature, which is already perfect, free, and sublime.

Anam Thubten

Note on Language Conventions

Tibetan words are presented in phonetics. While Anam Thubten's pronunciation is a Tibetan dialect from Golok, the phonetics in this text are the more commonly known Lhasa pronunciation for most terms. For Sanskrit terms, diacritics are omitted, and an "h" after "s" or "c" is added when the pronunciation requires it. In general, only the first occurrence of any foreign word is italicized.

Song of Realization

DUDJOM LINGPA

Song of Realization

མཆོག་སྤྲུལ་རྡོ་རྗེའི་ཞབས་ལ་ཕྱག་འཚལ་ལོ། །

སྣང་བ་བདེ་ཞིང་རྟོག་པ་གསལ་ཆིག་གིར། །
རྣམ་རྟོག་འོག་འགྱུའི་ཉོན་འབྱུང་དང་གིས་ཞི། །
ཧད་པོ་མ་ཡིན་ས་ལེར་གནས་པ་དེ། །
ཞི་གནས་ཆུམས་ཀྱི་མགོ་བྱུག་ལམ་ཧྲགས་རེས། །

བདེ་གསལ་མི་རྟོག་ཆུམས་ནི་གང་སྐྱེས་ཀྱང་། །
མི་ཆགས་མི་ཞེན་ཆེད་བསྒོམ་དོགས་སྤང་མིན། །
བདེན་བདེ་མཁའ་གསལ་ན་གསལ་མཁའ་སྟེ། །
རོ་བོ་ཆིད་ལས་རང་བཞིན་སྦྱོད་འདོད་མིན། །
བདེ་མཁའ་གསལ་མཁའ་གནས་མཁའ་དེ་ག་སྐྱོངས། །

Song of Realization

I pay homage to the feet of Padmasambhava.

Being happy; having a vividly clear mind;
the undercurrent of afflictive, deluded thoughts naturally dissolving;
not being blank; and abiding with clarity:
these are the beginning of shamatha experiences—definitive signs on the path.

Whatever experiences arise—be they bliss, clarity, or no-thought—
do not grasp, do not cling, do not deliberately meditate, and do not abandon due to fear.
When there is bliss, there is the experiencer of bliss; when there is clarity, there is the experiencer of clarity.
Apart from being in their essence, do not desire to engage with them as the nature [of mind].
Maintain that which is the experiencer of bliss or clarity, as it is.

Song of Realization

གང་ལ་གོལ་བསྒྲུམ་གོལ་ལམ་གྱི་གནད། །
ཕྱི་རུ་འཕྲོ་ཞིང་འཕྲོར་རྟོད་དང་སྟོང་མེལ། །
ནང་དུ་རྫོངས་འབྲིབས་རྒྱགས་འགྱོད་ཕྱི་ཚོམ་ལ། །
ཤེས་པ་ཁ་ཡན་པཿ ཀྱི་གསེང་ལ་བསྐྱམ། །
མཉམ་བཞག་ལྷུ་སྡུགས་འཛིན་འཆང་ཤིགས་ལ་ཞོག །
མི་ཡེངས་མི་བསྐྱམ་སྐྱོད་དེ་ཤིག་གེར་ཞོག །

རྗེས་ཐོབ་དུས་ཀྱང་དེ་བཞིན་དང་སྟོང་ཞིང་། །
ལྷ་སྐྱོད་འགྲོ་འདུག་ལས་ཀ་གང་བྱེད་ཀྱང་། །
རང་རོ་རིག་བཞིན་དན་ཤེས་སོ་མ་སྐྱོངས། །
ཡོད་མེད་བསམ་པའི་འཛིན་པ་གང་མེད་པས། །
མ་ཡེངས་ཡེངས་མེད་བསྐྱམ་སྐྱོངས་འཛིན་འཆང་མེད། །
དེའི་དང་མ་ཧོར་ཡིད་ལ་གང་བྱེད། །
གོལ་ནོར་ཧོར་ས་གང་ཡང་མེད་ཀྱུང་ཟད། །
དགེ་སྲིག་བླང་དོར་མ་ནོར་གནད་གཅིག་གོ །

སྤྱད་བྱེད་པོ་བདུད་འཛོམས་རྡོ་རྗེས་དགེ་མ་ཆོས་མཚོས་དོར་འབྲོས་ཕྱུག་མཁའ་འགྲོའི་འདུ་ཁང་དུ་བྲིས། །དགེའོ། །

Song of Realization

Not falling into any pitfalls and deceptions is a key point of the path.
When the mind goes outward and is scattered and restless, clear it by maintaining the natural state.
When the mind is lost inwardly in dullness, obscuration, regret, and doubt,
clear it by PHAD, and then meditate in that state.
Let go of grasping and fixation by resting in the manner of meditative equipoise.
Without distraction and without meditating, relax in the state of ease.

During post-meditation, one shall maintain the natural state like that.
In whatever you do—view, conduct, and all activities of going and staying—
maintain pristine mindfulness that is aware of its own nature.
There is no clinging to thoughts of existence or nonexistence.
Continue undistractedly the meditation that is already free from distraction, without clinging or grasping.
Do not lose that state, and do not conjure anything in your mind.
Then abide in the field where there are no more pitfalls, mistakes, and deviations.
The one key point is to unmistakenly know what to cultivate (virtues) and what to abandon (nonvirtues).

The stubborn beggar Dudjom Dorjé wrote these words at the request of the nun named Chötsho at the Dakini Gathering Hall Cave of Dröpuk. May it be auspicious.

Invoking the Blessings of the Lineage

མཚོ་སྐྱེས་རྡོ་རྗེའི་ཞབས་ལ་ཕྱག་འཚལ་ལོ། །

I pay homage to the feet of Padmasambhava.

I

Dzogchen Master Dudjom Lingpa

Dudjom Lingpa's mind was an inexhaustible treasury, a sea of wisdom teachings, each of which carries a liberating power. His teachings are not to be regarded as an intellectual work by an ordinary spiritual teacher but rather as the undiluted expression of the consciousness of someone who is truly awakened.

His works are often regarded as *terma*, or "revelatory writings." Usually, revelatory writings are works by *mahasiddha*s, or "enlightened masters," and are considered sublime because their source is not just the human intellect but an enlightened mind. Revelatory teachings and practices are a universal phenomenon that is not restricted to Tibetan Buddhism. Yet, due to various factors, including geography, culture, and history, the tradition of terma became especially popular and widely embraced in Tibet. In addition, terma are more often written by masters of the Nyingma lineage than by those from other lineages, and those terma are practiced by their followers.

Dudjom Lingpa was born in Eastern Tibet in 1835. He did not go through any formal monastic training, in contrast to many prominent Tibetan Buddhist teachers. Yet, at an early age, he became a well-known spiritual teacher. Dudjom Lingpa is unique in that, unlike many Tibetan masters, he is considered self-awakened. He didn't learn Dzogchen practices from a living human master but through meeting deities and masters in his visions, where he received their teachings and instructions.

His complete works are very diverse. The huge body of his literary work contains *sadhana*s (spiritual practices), meditation instructions, and *doha*s (songs of realization). His revelatory writings are often regarded as original and full of creativity. Some of his works have become very popular, such as the Tröma sadhana. When he was alive, he not only wrote prolifically but also taught extensively, attracting many monastics and laypeople to his teachings, many of whom became very respected Dharma teachers in their own right.

When someone reveals a terma, Buddhist scholars often analyze the authenticity of the work. They do not hesitate to criticize a terma if it is totally off-track regarding Buddhist doctrine. Dudjom Lingpa, who had never entered monastic training and never formally received Buddhist training, poured out an enormous amount of writings and teachings, drawing a lot of attention when he was alive. Yet some of the great contemporary scholars of the time gave a seal of approval to Dudjom Lingpa's termas, indicating their authenticity. Some of these scholars even became Dudjom Lingpa's disciples, including Khenpo Kunpal and Kyabgon Lingtrul.

Modern Relevance, Nonconceptual Wisdom

Dudjom Lingpa passed away at the beginning of the twentieth century in Tibet. He must have understood what was happening in the consciousness of the world and was able to predict its future state of mind. As a result, his teachings have practicality and relevance to people in today's world, especially when they are interpreted with clarity and skillfulness. One time, I was translating a very long text by Dudjom Lingpa, working with a few people in Richmond, California. We looked at each other with amazement as we read his words, as they sounded like he was from Northern California.

Not only are his teachings quite clear at a conceptual level to many people in the modern world, but they also resonate with people at an intuitive, energetic, and psychosomatic level. The revelatory writings of great masters like Dudjom Lingpa have a power to convey profundity that cannot be transmitted simply through words, language, or conceptualization. They can resonate and impact us just like good music. When someone plays good music, it doesn't matter whether you understand the lyrics or language; it can still affect you.

One time, I was visiting Madrid, Spain, and some people asked me what I might want to do while I was there. I said, "I'd like to see flamenco dancing." They took me to a small theater where there were three dancers and a group of singers. Watching them perform, I was transported into a magical realm. To me, it was utterly entertaining, but it was also somewhat transcendental because I forgot myself and all my troubles. The group of singers next to the dancers accompanied them with songs. I didn't understand one word, but it didn't matter. I felt that I understood intuitively what they were singing about, and their movements and songs had an impact that moved my heart. I think that Dudjom Lingpa's teachings can be regarded as an extraordinary song and dance that can impact you, whether or not you understand them conceptually.

In the nineteenth century, Tibet was a mystical and mysterious land for the Western world. There was little communication between Tibet and the outside world. As a visionary, Dudjom Lingpa seemed to know that someday his teachings would spread all over the world. One time, he was at Mardo Tashi Gyakhil in Golok, Eastern Tibet, at one of the highest altitudes in the world. It's a beautiful site situated between two rivers. There, he composed the Tröma sadhana, the most famous of his sadhanas. While his scribe was writing Dudjom Lingpa's spontaneous dictation, a wind blew and scattered the pages everywhere. Instead of being disturbed or annoyed, he said, "One day, this sadhana will go everywhere." Now, many thousands of people have started practicing his Tröma sadhana in Asia—Chinese, Tibetans, Bhutanese, and Nepalese. There's almost a "Tröma wave" spreading like wildfire. It's spreading in the West as well.

About Dzogchen

Even though Dzogchen has its own doctrine, its heart is beyond any kind of theory. It is about seeing the true nature of mind and reality in the realm of the here and now. In the Nyingma tradition, Dzogchen is regarded as the highest spiritual teaching and practice, pointing out the ultimate truth and giving the most direct path to enlightenment, or inner awakening. Many regard it as the shortcut to enlightenment. It does not take us on a spiritual zigzag journey of conceptual analysis and superfluous techniques but takes us straight to the heart of the matter.

Dzogchen regards itself as a system that transcends all other systems of spiritual teachings, practices, and disciplines. It enables us to experience nirvana, or enlightenment, without the need to adopt complex techniques and laborious spiritual disciplines. Many Buddhist schools of thought treat nirvana as an exalted state of consciousness that can only be actualized after a lengthy period of hard work, whereas Dzogchen points out that enlightenment can be actualized by simply realizing the pure nature of mind, or *rigpa*.

The premise of Dzogchen is that everyone has the potential to fully experience rigpa and become enlightened in this lifetime, and sometimes even in an immediate fashion. Rigpa is the unconditioned dimension of our consciousness that is always present in each of us, even before the ego develops. It is not some type of altered or exalted state of mind. Yet, it is often covered by all our thoughts, emotions, and habits, in the same way a beautiful nugget of gold can be covered by mud.

Dzogchen invites us to touch the very ground of reality by showing that mind, or consciousness, is the most important factor for our existence as well as for reality. It teaches that everything that we experience, including the separate self, is a display of our own consciousness. By realizing this, we can be freed naturally from the illusion of a separate self along with all the suffering that comes from not recognizing the illusion.

Dzogchen teaches that the mind is not solid and does not have a center, yet it is not totally nonexistent. Our sense of reality is like a dream phenomenon that is simply created by our own mind. When consciousness doesn't realize this, there is unending suffering because suffering is a mental creation and can never run out of fuel. Unlike the material world, where things do not run very well without fuel, the mind can continue to entertain itself with its grand and little stories until we stop it.

Sometimes, we can stop the mind's momentum immediately and jump into cosmic freedom and liberation. Then we feel we are no longer the egoic self but pure awareness, the sublime Primordial Buddha, which sees reality as an indescribable display of our own consciousness. It is an alive and breathing awakening that allows us to feel we have moved from imprisonment to freedom, from suffering to joy, from fear to love, from being self-centered to other-centered, and from ego to egolessness.

When consciousness realizes that all appearances are a display of itself, it is like waking up from a nightmarish dream that has always been lacking any solid ground. There is not even a dreamer when we recognize this. In that great epiphany, we begin to see that all our experiences are a display of something divine and utterly sublime, which is called rigpa.

The Dzogchen Lineage

Throughout history, Dzogchen has been mainly taught in the Nyingma lineage of Tibetan Buddhism. Its roots lie in India, where it was taught by masters such as Prahevajra, Manjushrimitra, and Shri Singha. In the eighth century, under the patronage of the Tibetan king Trisong Detsen, a throng of Indian masters came to Tibet, built monasteries, and taught Buddhism. Among them were Padmasambhava and Vimalamitra, both of whom taught Dzogchen to a group of disciples ready to understand it, including the king.

Many of their students became enlightened in their lifetime and taught Dzogchen to their own disciples. Eventually, it became a living spiritual lineage, which is still alive today.

Some of the most renowned Dzogchen masters include Longchenpa from the fourteenth century, Jigme Lingpa from the eighteenth century, and Dudjom Lingpa himself. There have also been very accomplished Dzogchen masters in our lifetime who are held in nearly the same esteem as those great masters, such as Chöje Jigme Phuntsok, Khenpo Munsel, and Lama Togden. They were truly awakened beings responsible for carrying the lineage with its full potency into today's world.

About the Doha

The doha in this book was composed by Dudjom Lingpa at an early stage of his life. He composed it in the Dröpuk cave in the Golok region, where he spent a lot of time practicing meditation before becoming a well-known master. Today, this cave is a pilgrimage site for many people. Some go simply to visit, while others may perform ceremonies or do a meditation retreat there.

Dudjom Lingpa's revelatory writings are imbued with the flavor of Dzogchen, whether they are sadhanas or meditation instructions. Some of his works on Dzogchen meditation are quite lengthy and require time and dedication to read and practice. This Dzogchen doha, however, is very appropriate for modern meditators. It is handy, pithy, practical, and encompasses the entire meditation practice from the Dzogchen point of view.

Meditation is a significant part of Dzogchen practice, not as a linear process of purifying or transforming our consciousness but as a means to drop into rigpa immediately. Therefore,

Dzogchen meditation is often called "meditation without meditation," "effortless meditation," or "uncontrived meditation."

Buddhist meditation practices generally fall into two categories: *shamatha* (calm abiding), known in Tibetan as *zhiné*; and *vipashyana* (direct seeing), or *lhaktong* in Tibetan. For anyone interested in meditation, especially Dzogchen, this doha offers a panoramic view of both.

Shamatha is a meditation practice where one experiences an undistracted state of mind that is serene. Vipashyana is commonly described as the direct seeing into the nature of reality. In Dzogchen, vipashyana can also refer to the direct experience of rigpa, or pure awareness, which is the unconditioned, true nature of mind.

This doha by Dudjom Lingpa describes not only the very nature of rigpa but also the meditation practices that allow one to experience it in the most direct way. How could you not love this doha? As someone who is a big fan of Dudjom Lingpa, simply reading this doha opens my heart, intoxicating it with joy.

2

Devotion: The Path to Freedom

Our human mind is an unfathomable mystery even to ourselves. We tend to think we know everything about it, yet perhaps we are just scratching the surface. This, of course, is kind of ironic. It is like saying that what is closest to us is also unknown to us.

There is a place in our consciousness that can be an inexhaustible source of creativity and is saturated with love and compassion. Whenever we have a moment to arrive at that place, sacred creativity flows without any effort. There is even an expression in the Dzogchen tradition: "the sudden eruption of an expanse of wisdom and compassion." This expression describes the experience that sometimes happens when meditators reach a state where their mind is totally free from internal conditioning. From that state, a river of sacred creativity overflows, and they are able to teach and write effortlessly. What flows out of their consciousness at that time is not even a product of learned knowledge.

Dudjom Lingpa is the epitome of this marvelous yet human phenomenon. Even though he was not a traditional monk who went through monastic training in the Buddhist doctrines, he was able to deliver profound sermons and compose extraordinary teachings that inspired laypeople and scholars alike. One could say that Dudjom Lingpa wrote not from the state of the usual intellect but from the state of consciousness called the *dharmakaya* mind, or the mind of the Buddha.

The Purpose of an Homage

Dudjom Lingpa begins this doha with an homage. Tibetan Buddhist masters often write an homage at the beginning of a text to a master or deity that they have utmost love toward. This has become the standard for any sacred Tibetan writing. It helps the author feel that they are in touch with a state of mind that is not tainted by ego, ulterior motives, or even the realm of the intellect. It is also a way to bless their work so that it will have the positive power to transform the minds of those who come across it.

In the Tibetan style of writing, paying homage sets the tone for the entire text. Here, Dudjom Lingpa is paying homage to the feet of Padmasambhava, who has many names. Sometimes he is called Tsokye Dorje in Tibetan or Padma Vajra in Sanskrit, which means Lake-Born Vajra. Often, he is referred to as Guru Rinpoche, the precious master.

Paying homage to Padmasambhava indicates that the theme of this text is related to Vajrayana or Dzogchen. Padmasambhava is a tantric master who brought Vajrayana and Dzogchen to Tibet in the eighth century. If not for him, Buddhism most likely would not have taken root in the land of Tibet.

Padmasambhava is loved by Tibetans and regarded as one of the three protectors, along with Avalokiteshvara and Tara, of

Devotion: The Path to Freedom

the Land of Snow, the poetic name for Tibet. He is exalted in the hearts of Tibetans to the level of a Buddha, serving as a focus for Tibetan people who practice the path of devotion, which is a powerful act of surrendering the ego into love.

As a yogi in the Nyingma lineage, which is the tradition of Padmasambhava, Dudjom Lingpa had unflinching love for Padmasambhava. Many regard Dudjom Lingpa as a regent of Padmasambhava, someone who acts as his representative to the world. It is said that many of Dudjom Lingpa's students felt that being in his presence was like being in the presence of Padmasambhava himself and hearing his profound teachings.

A Nondual Homage

Even though this homage appears to be one simple sentence of praise, it is much more profound than it may seem. This is not just about Dudjom Lingpa pledging his allegiance to Padmasambhava. Instead, he is expressing the highest level of devotion—not ordinary love, but love in which the heart is free from all resistance and the mind itself, both of which can hinder the path to freedom.

The true spirit of this homage also goes beyond any ideas we may have about paying homage, which are often constructed around duality: there is an object to be worshipped, there is a worshipper, and there is an act of worship. That kind of devotion has a deep sense of separation between oneself and the beloved. This seems to be the basis of devotion in many religious traditions, and there is nothing wrong with it. But it is stuck in the realm of duality.

Here, this homage is what is called in the Tantric Buddhist tradition "the homage of the nondual view." We pay homage with the understanding that there is no separation between the worshipper and the object of worship. This can appear very radical to many because our mind is often in the habitual trap of duality, even when we are doing spiritual practices. It is very easy for our mind to feel a separation between ourselves and the divine. But the true meaning of this homage is that there is no separation between ourselves and Padmasambhava, the true guru who lies within us and who is essentially our own true nature.

This notion that the true guru does not lie outside but is another name for our own true nature is expressed in the poetry of the Fifth Dalai Lama (seventeenth century). In his homage to Padmasambhava, he says,

> In the center of the heart, within the youthful vase body,
>   primordially present,
> resides self-knowing awareness, the true Padmasambhava.
> Having recognized one's own true nature, no other guru
> is sought elsewhere; to this inseparable, single essence, I
>   prostrate!

In Dzogchen, the true guru, or *rang rig dön gyi lama*, is the same as pure awareness, which is the true nature of our own mind or being. The ultimate guru does not lie outside ourselves. Our own pure awareness is the ultimate guru.

Knowing the true nature of our mind is considered the peak of all spiritual epiphanies in Dzogchen. There is no insight that goes beyond it. Knowing this is almost the end of the spiritual quest, since there is nothing to seek beyond that and nothing to be known beyond that, whether you call it the Absolute, the Truth, or something else.

And yet, when this truth is realized, it is not that our intellect figured out something profound, which often involves a duality between that which is known and the knower. This duality is what we usually experience when we know something. It is the foundation not only of knowledge in our worldly life but also of most spiritual knowledge. However, the true knowing of the nature of mind is not knowledge acquired by intellect—it is an experience of knowing the depth of our being that is as direct as tasting the sweetness of honey. That experience creates an immediate impact, which often releases the knot of our mind—the ego structure with all its concepts and karmic patterns.

The Path of Devotion

The devotional path is one of the principal practices in Tibetan Buddhism, especially in relation to the guru, who is the focal point of such practice. One could say there are two major doorways to inner freedom: the mind and the heart. The devotional practice is a direct path to freedom through the heart. Tibetan yogis often practice rituals or sadhanas through which they cultivate love toward the guru. The goal of such practice is to eventually feel that the very object of love is no longer outside but is indeed one's true nature, which is already liberated, already Buddha.

Vajrayana emphasizes the importance of developing a devotion-based relationship with the guru as a key factor in one's awakening. Not only can one learn so much from the guru, but the relationship is also a medium through which one can learn to open the heart and surrender the ego. Surrendering the ego can sometimes be very challenging because it feels like we are surrendering to somebody. But in this context, it is filled with wisdom and is not about surrendering to someone outside ourselves. It is more about learning how to let go of the ego and developing love at a transcendent level.

Even though Dudjom Lingpa did not have any human guru, he had unflinching, heartfelt devotion to the gurus of the Dzogchen lineage who lived before him, such as Padmasambhava and Longchen Rabjam. This very line of homage is indeed his heartfelt proclamation of devotion toward Padmasambhava.

Once, Chöje Jigme Phuntsok, the founder of the largest Buddhist monastery in the world, built a big throne and had all the monks line up holding banners, as if to welcome a very important guest or esteemed Buddhist master. But then he asked the monks to bring one of his texts and place it on the throne. He then said, "This is my *tulku*." In Tibet, when a master dies, a tulku is someone recognized by the community as a reincarnation of that master who will carry on their spiritual legacy.

Let's imagine that this doha is Dudjom Lingpa's tulku, carrying his vision to awaken the hearts and minds of beings through the wisdom of Dzogchen. The homage is the face of the tulku who we are now seeing with our own eyes in this moment.

The Art of Stillness

སྤྲང་བ་བདེ་ཞིང་རྟོག་པ་གསལ་ཐིག་གེར། །
རྣམ་རྟོག་འོག་འགྱུའི་ཉོན་འཁྲུལ་རང་གིས་ཞི། །
ཧད་པོ་མ་ཡིན་ས་ལེར་གནས་པ་དེ། །
ཞི་གནས་ཉམས་ཀྱི་མགོ་བཟུག་ལམ་རྟགས་རེས། །

Being happy; having a vividly clear mind;
the undercurrent of afflictive, deluded thoughts
   naturally dissolving;
not being blank; and abiding with clarity:
these are the beginning of shamatha experiences—
   definitive signs on the path.

3

Understanding the Mind

For a long time, meditation was a property of religion, often linked in our mind with a religious tradition and the holy observance of the spiritual elite, such as monks and nuns. Yet meditation does not belong to any one particular tradition and cannot be defined as a singular practice. It has been present throughout history and used for various objectives, such as a medium between people and an external divinity.

Buddhist meditation is distinguished from many other forms of religious practice. Its goal is not communion with the divine but rather to change and transform one's consciousness through one's own effort. One could say that the Buddha and Buddhist meditations are the epitome of the Axial Age.

The Axial Age refers to a few centuries before the Common Era when humanity went through a major inner revolution and evolution. It was a time when humanity realized that they had the ability to transform themselves, and their fate was not always dependent on the mercy of deities looking down on them from behind the clouds. This was also the time when great spiritual masters and thinkers came into the world, such as Buddha, Lao Tse, and Socrates. It was, in its own way, an age of enlightenment, even though we don't call it that. The inner evolution from the Axial Age continues even now with surprising advances.

In today's world, meditation is often understood as a discipline that involves inner work to change the state of one's mind, improve oneself, or develop the noble capacities of the mind. Meditation is also used to explore the dimension of reality that is often unrecognized by the lens of the ordinary mind, a mind filtered by our thoughts and opinions.

So the idea of exploring the mind is not only a religious or spiritual matter. One doesn't need to be formally religious or spiritual to be deeply interested in a practice such as meditation. This is why, in today's world, there is a small but growing number of people from different walks of life who don't fit into the traditional ideas of being spiritual or religious. Yet they are sincerely interested in and actively practicing some form of meditation.

Attending to the Mind

The mind is a realm in which we can find the actual root of all our problems as well as the true remedy for solving them. It is also a realm where a person can encounter peak human experiences, such as self-transcendence and universal love. So there is every reason we should pay attention to the mind. A huge bulk of Buddhist practice is about paying attention to our mind, understanding it, and learning how to change it.

However, we are busy every day paying attention to everything else—what we eat, the clothes we wear, the problems to be solved, and so on. Such attention is, of course, necessary for our very survival. Through such a scope of attention, we may find a thousand things are wrong with ourselves, our house, or whatever, and we may try to fix the problems. Luckily, we often find the right remedies to change the conditions that don't agree with us. More and more, this habit of finding problems and fixing them has become the basis of our modern way of life.

This strategy has two goals. One is, of course, to continue to exist. The second is to achieve happiness. The first goal is universal. Even animals are busy in their own realm, trying to survive. Look at a squirrel—she is very hardworking. You don't find a lazy squirrel who sleeps late and doesn't show up for work. Squirrels are extremely diligent in many ways. They pick up all the acorns from the oak trees in the proper season, and they know how to store them as food by burying them. Later, they know exactly where the acorns are stored.

Animals also have challenges, but they find remedies to overcome their struggles in order to survive. However, it is not with the idea that they will be happy if they have a lot of acorns. It seems that their impulse is not driven by the desire to be happy but by the desire to exist.

Whereas we humans are very complex creatures, partly because we possess consciousness that allows us to think, imagine, and construct stories. As a result, we have a strong sense of self, or ego structure, that gives rise to powerful feelings, passions, and impulses, such as ambition, greed, or even a sense of a goal to be achieved. Therefore, unlike squirrels or other animals, most of our activities are actually driven by the powerful motivation to achieve this thing called happiness.

Releasing the Knot of the Mind

Yet, happiness comes from inside, a source that is much more reliable and not dependent on outer conditions. It comes purely from the right state of our own mind. So there is a blind spot in the human strategy to find happiness, not realizing that happiness is an internal experience related to the mind. In other words, we are looking for happiness in the wrong place.

We believe that if we solve lots of problems, such as disease or physical discomfort, and create a maximum level of comfort and security—such as having the right food, the best place to live, or enough money—we will be happy forever. This is like a donkey chasing after a dangling carrot. Sooner or later, we have to wake up. This strategy is not really working; it's not paying off.

Eventually, this becomes a very palpable reality, and yet, people have such strong resistance to admitting that their strategy in the pursuit of happiness is not working. So, we humans continue to use this old strategy to try to capture happiness from outer circumstances. This becomes a completely futile endeavor since happiness is truly a state of our own mind.

The Buddhist Perspective on the Mind

Buddha realized this very fact, and his entire teaching revolves around finding inner freedom through working with our minds. He also saw that, in general, the human mind is full of potential but is also very unruly and confused. He even used metaphors to describe the unruliness of the human mind, such as an untamed wild horse or a crazy elephant, pointing out how dangerous the mind can be to ourselves and to the world.

Buddha saw that the human mind is totally confused when it comes to the nature of reality, as well as intoxicated by very powerful forces such as jealousy, greed, hatred, and so forth. He saw that ultimately, most problems in the world, including war, violence, and mental suffering, stem from this unruly human mind. The mind is, if not the sole, the primary cause of all human woes. Buddha cut to the chase by stating that our mind can be our worst enemy because it can harm us more than anyone else. It can also be our best friend because it can help us more than anyone else.

This wise understanding of the power of the mind is utterly simple, as well as brilliant and accurate. There is not much to argue against. We can see this is true through our own life experiences. If our mind is troubled, regardless of the life condition we are in, we can end up being quite miserable.

That's not the end of the story. When we are miserable, we then cause problems for other people as well. Whereas if we have gained mastery over our mind, it is like finding the holy grail; we tap into an inexhaustible resource of peace, joy, and even transcendence. The mind is the very faculty through which we experience everything, including being alive. Even the two most important human experiences—happiness and suffering—are states of our mind. Our quality of life is not always determined by external situations, such as our career, the neighborhood where we live, our financial situation, and even our health. It is often determined by what we do with our mind.

Therefore, we should be very interested in the workings and the very nature of the mind. Through such knowledge, we will find the means to work with our mind and bring about experiences that can be regarded as transcendent. If we don't attend to the mind, we may completely miss its extraordinary capacity.

Taming the Mind

Buddha's approach to taming one's mind is to treat it as an unruly beast running amok. Taming the mind is one of the fundamental goals of Buddhist practitioners. There is a verse chanted by many Buddhists to remind themselves of the heart of their spiritual practice, which says,

> One shall not commit anything unwholesome;
> One shall cultivate the perfectly wholesome;
> One shall tame one's own mind.
> This is the way of the Buddha.

When people recite this verse, either at temples or in their homes, they are reminded that their true practice is to tame their own mind. Buddha also said that the mind is the forerunner of all things, including our deeds and actions in the world. This indicates that no matter how much we try to change ourselves externally by being good or noble, unless we also change our mind, we will not be transformed at our core level.

Now, what does it mean to tame our mind? It means to gain mastery over our own mind and not be ruled by powerful thoughts and emotions, especially negative ones. It also involves increasing the sense of our inner goodness, such as love and joy.

Up to now, we have been delivering bad news about the human mind, but there is also good news: intrinsically, it is very flexible. This is also validated by modern science. Both science and Buddhism say that the mind is quite malleable and is not as static and resistant to change as it may appear.

There are many incredible individuals who prove this statement to be true. Some people go through tragedies or lose everything, yet they don't lose heart. They shine as great models for humanity because of their ability to stay positive and see the bright side of life. Some of them are able to transcend all challenges.

A Source of Inspiration

My spiritual master, Lama Tsurlo, is someone who went through many difficulties in his life, some of which were even catastrophic. He had health issues at a very early age, and later he became disabled after developing a spinal deformity.

According to oral stories, when Lama Tsurlo was young, he was taken for healing to Anam Chatralwa, who was an early student of Dudjom Lingpa and had a hermitage at Takyak Mountain in Eastern Tibet.

There's a humorous anecdote about that visit. When they met, Anam Chatralwa told Lama Tsurlo to do prostrations and count them using a *mala* (prayer beads), and then gave him his own mala. During one of the breaks in his practice, Lama Tsurlo put the mala down, and suddenly a large bird swooped down and took the mala. Later, Lama Tsurlo told me he had so much regret for losing the mala. But he said it with a big smile, as if he thought the whole thing was very amusing.

In some ways, you could say Lama Tsurlo was an unlucky guy because of all his health issues. On the other hand, he was a very lucky person, as he entered the Buddhist path and studied with a well-known master, Apang Terton. Later in his life, he became a well-loved Buddhist teacher to many people, including a well-known female guru, Tare Lhamo. He lived as a lifelong hermit, spending most of his time in solo meditation retreat, with little in the way of material possessions. When he died, he left only a few things, such as calligraphy of texts and a few cups. Yet in his presence, I never felt any sense of poverty. I felt he was very rich inside and content.

To me, he was a transcender who went beyond all worldly concerns. I felt that he could not be shaken by difficult situations that might throw many other people off balance. I felt he was deeply happy, but not in a "happy-go-lucky" way. He has been a source of inspiration to me and others, even though he is no longer in this world. If there were a happiness contest in the world, most likely Lama Tsurlo would win the medal for that. His life teaches us that the quality of life is not necessarily determined by the circumstances we inevitably go through but by our ability to work with our mind. His life stands as a testimony to the potential of inner work and meditation practice.

This is a very inspiring finding, which can give us hope and aspiration for inner growth. There are countless testimonials from people who have gone through major changes in themselves, which we may call inner transformation. Many of them used Buddhist meditation techniques to work with their mind.

The ultimate goal of Buddhist meditation practice is to set ourselves free from the genesis of all our problems, which, surprisingly, does not lie outside but rather in our state of mind that is trapped in its own creation.

The Concept of Prapancha: Mental Proliferation

A large percentage of human suffering and problems in the world are a product of what is called *prapancha* in Sanskrit and *tröpa*

Understanding the Mind

in Tibetan, which means "conceptual proliferation." It indicates that our suffering is not always physical but often mental and conceptual. This appears to be unique to human beings, as we are able to think and conceptualize.

There is obviously suffering in the kingdoms of other species, such as birds, animals, and insects, who go through struggles like hunger and pain. Yet human beings suffer in a unique way because we have the capacity to think and construct storylines about ourselves, the world, and the situations that we encounter.

It is not that there is something wrong with having thoughts or mental activity. This mental activity is required in everyday life, even to perform simple functions like getting in the car, cooking food, or dialing a phone number. But the point is that our mind is always wandering with repetitive mental chatter, which we can call prapancha. Most thoughts that pop up in our mind are not particularly creative or original. The mind is just repeating all its habits unconsciously, which takes us away from connecting with the present moment and prevents us from getting in touch with a more sublime, spiritual state of mind like rigpa.

This human mind is the most extraordinary thing in the entire cosmos. The cosmos itself would not be considered extraordinary without a human mind. Who would think the cosmos is extraordinary in the first place? I have a dog named Chloe who sometimes wants to go out at night. Obviously, she is not looking at the stars or having a religious experience, seeing how amazing the universe is. Most likely, she smells some critters that she wants to bark at.

But when I go out at night, I occasionally have moments where I am so humbled and moved by seeing how divinely exquisite this universe is—a vast sky filled with immeasurable heavenly bodies such as the stars, the moon, and the planets. When we think something is extraordinary, our mind perceives it that way—anything extraordinary or holy is not inherently so. The sense of beauty, the extraordinary, and holiness are not absolute properties; they are all based on human perception.

Many of our struggles seem to exist in the dimension of our mind. Yet, when we look into the natural world, it is also filled with physical hardships. However, we may find there is also a deep peace in the natural world because it is devoid of the human suffering caused by the thinking mind. For example, we might see a nest created by birds in the forest, and as long as no other creatures bother it, the bird seems to be happy with its nest. We don't see one bird depressed by thinking that another bird's nest is bigger or more beautiful.

On the other hand, we human beings have so many psychological woes from constructing the sense of self. We become aware of that virtual version of who we are, then we identify with it, and ultimately, we praise or judge it. When we praise it, we become arrogant. When we judge it, powerful experiences like self-hatred and self-loathing are created, leading to unbearable mental pain.

Prapancha encompasses all the concepts and opinions that have become the building blocks of our perceived reality. The problem is that prapancha is conditioned by a fundamental ignorance about the nature of reality. We experience each day from a state of consciousness fueled by that ignorance. In other words, even though we are under the impression that we are seeing and interacting with reality, this is merely a universal delusion that we collectively believe in.

Freedom from Prapancha

The true nature of reality itself can only be seen when we drop mental proliferation. The state of reality free from prapancha is called *trödrel* in Tibetan, or *nisprapancha* in Sanskrit. Going beyond mental proliferation is regarded as the highest inner liberation. When we experience that state, a whole host of our problems will dissolve immediately, just like waking up from a bad dream.

One of the main purposes of Dzogchen is to drop into that state of freedom in the present moment. Therefore, some hymns and prayers praise the freedom from mental proliferation, trödrel, as the ultimate guru or ultimate Buddha. People use these prayers to develop a strong aspiration to experience that state.

In today's world, when someone who went through many struggles dies, people often comment that their death was a freedom from all their suffering. To me, this is not a very inspiring idea. I don't think we have to wait for death to be released from the miseries of this life. To me, trödrel is a beautiful form of death while living. It is the death of the ego and the death of ignorance and delusions. We may want to welcome that ego death rather than count on physical death as an exit from life's challenges.

In the true sense, the most powerful spiritual experiences are not just a form of inner death but also birth. It is death because in such experiences, we feel we die to our old identity, all the mental stories, and even our suffering. It is also birth because we do not end up with an existential nothingness that is boring and leaves us thinking, "Now what?" It is birth because we feel we are a new being, reincarnated with a sense of deep joy and an understanding of the higher purpose of life. We feel that now, the journey to live life fully has begun. There is a sense of flourishing.

Releasing the Knot of the Mind

Dzogchen points out that this experience of trödrel, freedom from mental proliferation, is not an unreachable, extramundane state of our consciousness. We can drop into this state at any given moment. Therefore, all the Dzogchen meditation practices are designed to help us experience it, either directly or indirectly.

4

The Practice of Shamatha

One of the primary meditation practices in Buddhism is shamatha, or calm abiding. This is the initial step in the endeavor to tame one's mind. The default state of one's mind is usually quite noisy and sometimes even gripped by internal disturbances, from anxiety to negative self-talk. Shamatha practice is about applying concentration to quiet one's mind.

The Environment

Traditional meditation manuals recommend being in optimal conditions to practice shamatha meditation. This could be a quiet environment, such as a hermitage in the mountains or forest, where there is not so much busy human activity to distract one's mind. It is also recommended not to interact with too many people, which can pull us back into our usual reactive patterns. Sometimes, people are encouraged to observe silence as a support for the practice of shamatha.

In these modern days, most people don't have the right circumstances to go on a long meditation retreat frequently. Perhaps many will have a chance to do a weeklong or monthlong meditation retreat once or twice in their lives. But this should not be a cause for discouragement. Shamatha can be practiced in almost every environment, including our own homes.

Daily Habit

In general, we can make meditation practice our daily habit. Once it is built into our daily life, it becomes very natural for us. This is true for all our daily rituals. Think about brushing your teeth. Imagine you grew up in a culture where people don't brush their teeth. For them, brushing their teeth might appear strange, uncomfortable, and an extraneous effort. But in modern cultures, for many people, brushing their teeth is part of basic daily hygiene. They don't even think about it; they do it almost automatically. But we are not born with such a habit; it is acquired by training. There is a name for the trainer: it is called a "parent."

This tells us that almost anything can be built into our system as a habit. If one starts practicing meditation every day, even for a short period, eventually it becomes part of one's daily life. Then, starting the day with either a short or long period of meditation will have a positive impact on one's mind for the rest of the day.

We have the idea that we are going to practice meditation to "change our life." But what is life if not every day? If we don't engage with daily action, then changing our life is just a big idea or wishful thinking that remains a grand personal project, and yet nothing comes out of it. Therefore, *today* is always the perfect time to practice meditation.

Intention

Before we begin the actual shamatha practice, we might recite an entire liturgy or some inspiring verses to invoke the right intention. This will help us develop the primary motivation for why we are doing this practice. In the Tibetan Buddhist tradition, most spiritual practices are built upon one single motivation—to become enlightened, not just for oneself but for everyone. Such motivation is called *bodhichitta*, or "awakened heart." Here, even though shamatha is a method to still our mind, in the context of this Dzogchen doha, it must be built upon bodhichitta, a non-egoic motivation.

Dzogchen meditation is not meant to be done with a worldly intention, such as to simply calm our mind or reduce stress. In today's world, many things have been co-opted and commercialized, which is like an invasive force in this modern culture that touches everything, including meditation practice. In some cases, there may be individuals or institutions that use Buddhist meditation to fulfill very mundane goals.

For example, employees might be able to focus more and have less stress to maximize their productivity, or military personnel may use meditation to sharpen their focus during combat. Therefore, in today's world, we may have ethical issues about such meditation practices. I am not saying that these uses of meditation are intrinsically bad, but this is not the goal of shamatha in the context of Dudjom Lingpa's teachings.

Our Ineffable Impulse

There is a mystery about why we even have the impulse to meditate in the first place. One may be very curious to know where such a thought arises from. It is even more mysterious why that intention arises in the mind of some and not in others. There could be all kinds of explanations, including environmental conditions. For example, growing up in a culture where people meditate may influence you.

But it is more than just the environment; it may be karmic, too. Even some people who go to a monastery may not want to meditate. Two people who grow up in the same environment may differ. One may carry meditation into their daily life, while the other has no interest in it whatsoever. So it is a complete mystery.

Ultimately, the source of the intention to meditate is ineffable. This very topic is mentioned by the eighth-century master Shantideva in his text, *The Way of the Bodhisattva*:

> Just as in the night, in the darkness dense with clouds,
> lightning momentarily reveals the light,
> so too, by the power of the Buddha,
> occasionally, the minds of beings are momentarily inclined
> to merit.

This verse says that we human beings experience virtuous thoughts, such as the intention to meditate, due to the power of the Buddha. But the Buddha here can be interpreted as our inner Buddha, or the unborn Buddha, the enlightened nature of our consciousness. It means all our virtuous thoughts, including the intention to meditate, come from our inner Buddha, which wants to wake up to itself.

The Practice of Shamatha

Meditation Posture

When we meditate, whether shamatha or something else, posture is the first thing to learn. In the past, people always sat in a cross-legged posture while meditating. This may be because in many older cultures, people didn't sit on chairs. That being said, a cross-legged posture has some intrinsic benefits for our mind while meditating. It can help prevent a variety of physical discomforts and allow us to feel that our energy flows easily through our bodies. But this should not be turned into a draconian guideline; sitting on a chair is also an option.

After sitting down, it is good to take some time to adjust our posture, such as having our back straight. This has an immediate impact on our body and mind, allowing us to feel dignified and grounded at the center of our being. We may even feel that being grounded is a form of equilibrium—nothing can challenge us, shake us, or throw us off-balance. Whatever might arise—internal challenges like thought and emotions, or even disturbances from outside—nothing can take us from equilibrium.

This feeling of being completely grounded in the unshakable center of our being is similar to the way Buddha sat under the bodhi tree. He vowed that he would not get up until he became enlightened, no matter what happened. Buddha said,

> Though this body may wither and dry up,
> though the skin and bones that compose it may crumble,
> until I have attained enlightenment, difficult to find after many eons,
> I will not move my body from this seat.

Releasing the Knot of the Mind

It is said that while Buddha sat in that posture with the determination not to give in to any challenges until his mind was illuminated, a variety of challenges arose. He encountered very powerful emotions and thoughts, often depicted as the army of Mara that attacked him. Yet Buddha did not run away. He sat in that sense of being grounded, and the challenges dissolved by themselves, leading him to perfect awakening.

As part of our posture, we let our shoulders relax, which gives a sense of ease so that we are not uptight or rigid. Even though we are grounded in dignity and equilibrium, our whole energy is not so rigid and flows with ease. Without trying hard to be dignified, there is a feeling of effortlessness everywhere in our being—no struggle in our body and mind.

Then we can join our hands or rest them on our knees. In Buddhism, the way we place our hands is regarded as a *mudra* (sacred gesture), which has significance. For example, joining our hands on our lap is called the "mudra of equanimity." Resting our hands on our knees is called "resting in the pristine nature of one's mind," or *semnyi ngalsö chakgya*. This is the most popular hand gesture in the Dzogchen tradition.

We will discover that our physical posture influences our mood and even our state of mind in an immediate fashion. There is a notion that simply by sitting in the right posture, meditation will happen naturally, which is often evident in our own experience. The traditional meditation postures are designed to bring about dignity, stillness, and ease.

Not only can our physical posture influence our mind but even our facial expressions can have an effect. Research has shown that simply smiling can actually release serotonin. In the sacred images of Buddha, he smiles as an expression of no struggle and being at ease. So it might be nice to put a gentle smile around our mouth and eyes at the beginning of shamatha meditation. For shamatha, we can leave our eyes open or close them.

Settling In

It's good to take a few moments to settle into the body, which is a wonderful doorway to the present moment. If we remember to feel our bodily sensations, we will also be in the present moment more often in our everyday life. By settling into the sensations in our body, we can pull our attention back from the mental realm of fantasies, opinions, self-talk, rumination, and endless stories, which create an almost virtual reality, a pure expression of prapancha.

When we settle into the body, we can feel we are here—we are at home. Notice that by feeling "at home"—the true home that is our own being—we sense a wholesome quality in our being. Our mind is no longer scattered or fragmented. The experience is like a somatic meditation that comes naturally from the posture and quiets our whole system.

Concentration on the Breath

We can use different things for the object of concentration. Traditionally, the breath is one of the main objects of concentration in shamatha practice. Regarding the concentration on breath, it is not that we have to do anything extra. We are breathing all the time, even though we are not conscious of it. While we are walking, even while we are sleeping, we are always breathing, so there is no need for any conscious effort. Breathing is the natural rhythm of our body. Here we simply pay attention to it.

The key point of this practice is that we don't lose concentration on the breath. For this reason, sometimes people use the method of counting their breath. Some people count the in-breath up to any number between five and ten. But counting is not necessary if you don't have any difficulty following your breath.

You can follow your breath as it reaches the tip of your nose or be aware of the changing temperature at the nostrils. You can also feel the rhythm, sensations, and movements that naturally arise with each breath. You can notice that when you breathe in, your shoulders rise and your belly expands, and when you breathe out, your shoulders drop down and your belly contracts. You can also notice all the other subtle physical sensations that occur along the pathway of each breath.

Usually, with such concentration, the space for thoughts in our mind is reduced. You will experience an inner silence where there are not so many thoughts. If you follow one thought, your attention can be hijacked by it, leading to a train of thoughts that can go on forever. So whenever a thought occurs during concentration, immediately remember to return to the breath.

Concentration on Sensations

We can also concentrate on physical sensations, which are available all the time. Like the breath, they also don't require any extra effort. Sensations are always happening in our bodies, but in general, we are often not aware of them. We tend to live in the dimension of the thinking mind. But there is so much value at many levels in being in touch with the physical sensations of the body. The moment we bring our attention to the sensations in our body, we immediately unplug from the trap of the thinking mind and all its mental chatter. In that very moment, we stop letting the thinking mind traumatize us over and over again. There is a sense of returning home with immediate stillness and peace.

There are formal ways of concentrating on bodily sensations, but we can also find opportunities to concentrate on physical sensations and find inner stillness throughout the day. For example, sitting on a chair, we can bring gentle attention to the feeling of our feet touching the ground or to the sensations in our belly, chest, or hands.

Some friends of mine shared a technique where every now and then during the day, you can press the tip of each finger with your thumb sequentially and pay attention to that. This is a very simple but useful method to unhook our attention from that wild thinking mind.

Other Objects of Concentration

The object of concentration can also include ordinary objects and sounds, as well as sacred objects, such as images of buddhas, deities, and mantric syllables. The sacred images can be physical representations, such as paintings, or can be inner visualizations.

One of the most popular concentration practices is visualizing Buddha in your mind. The image of Buddha is more than just the physical representation of some historical person. It is also designed as an object of meditation that can invoke experiences such as calmness. This is quite easy to understand by simply observing the image of Buddha, who is golden in color, sits in a lotus posture, and has a gentle smile. That image has an intrinsic power to invoke calmness, in the same way a beautiful rose can create waves of joy in our hearts when we see it. People find that by concentrating on the image of Buddha, they often feel two states of mind: calmness and joy.

Both the form and the sounds of mantras can be objects of concentration, either by reciting mantras, looking at mantric syllables placed in front of you, or visualizing them in your mind. You can also concentrate on ordinary sounds as well as sacred ones.

One time, I led a silent, residential meditation retreat in a beautiful valley in the US state of Idaho during the winter, which is magnificently enchanting at that time of year. The high mountains and grounds are covered with white snow, and there is deafening silence everywhere. The trees are there to keep you company.

At one point, noise was coming from the kitchen, most likely a refrigerator. At first, I reacted, thinking there should not be disturbing noises in this pristine meditation environment. But there was nothing I could do. Then I decided to concentrate on the noise instead of reacting. I found that it was extremely calming to concentrate on it. I noticed my mind didn't get distracted by thoughts, and the concentration brought me calmness and joy, which might seem very strange given that object. Now and then, a thought would arise, and I would begin to engage with it. But in the middle of indulging in the stream of thoughts, the sound would arise and bring me back to the present moment. Later, whenever the sound came, I became happy, as if I were anticipating it. This is an example of how ordinary things can be an object of the concentration practice.

The Practice of Shamatha

Supreme Shamatha

Many Dzogchen masters tend to encourage their students not to fixate on long periods of shamatha meditation that is based on narrowing attention on a particular object. Instead, they teach students to relax without focusing on a particular object, let the doors of the senses remain open, without judging what arises in one's meditation and especially without following one's thoughts. This is called *supreme shamatha*, or *chok gi zhiné*. The term distinguishes this type of shamatha from other forms of shamatha, which often involve exerting effort to narrowly pin down the mind on a particular object.

In many ways, this is similar to open awareness meditation, which we will describe later. The only difference is that in supreme shamatha, we are still encouraged to feel the calmness that arises in such a relaxing posture, and intentionally and gently anchor the mind in that stillness.

Some Dzogchen masters might say that you don't need such a practice because shamatha and open awareness are just one practice, which is true in many ways. But wise Dzogchen masters also say that, in general, most people may need the practice of supreme shamatha as a different technique from open awareness so that their mind becomes more tamed. Otherwise, without such training, if people try to drop into rigpa directly, most likely the wind of wild thoughts and internal turbulence will just carry them away. They will not be able to remain in rigpa at all.

When you read this doha, it doesn't describe the precise shamatha practices such as concentration, nor does it create an obvious demarcation between shamatha and open awareness. It simply describes Dzogchen meditation, which is all about relaxing in the natural state of your mind. Then supreme shamatha naturally develops in one's mind, which evolves into open awareness. One should bear in mind that the form of shamatha mentioned in this doha refers only to the supreme shamatha.

An Accessible Practice

The methodology of shamatha can be quite simple; it doesn't invoke any complex system. There are no lengthy prerequisites for it. The beauty of shamatha is that almost anyone can start practicing it right away. It is all about directing your attention away from your thinking mind by replacing it with attention to an object.

As we continue to practice shamatha meditation, we will see its effect more and more. Not only are we able to enjoy stillness while we are meditating, but life outside the meditation period will be positively impacted by it.

5

Shamatha Experiences

After settling into a posture and focusing on an object of concentration, we can soon feel a wonderful sense of being still and calm; time seems to stop. There are many similes to describe the calmness we experience. It is like the peace that can be discovered in the pristine natural world, such as in the mountains or forests untouched by the hustle and bustle of human civilization.

Undoubtedly, nature has the power to invoke such inner serenity, allowing us to feel we are in harmony with everything—the world, life, reality—and our whole being is resting at ease. Yet the truth is that without going into the forest or mountains, we can experience such calmness through shamatha practice. This inner calmness can be regarded as an oasis or sanctuary in which we are free from the disturbances of the mind. We can call it the inner hermitage.

A hermitage is usually in the forest, mountains, or wilderness, which lies beyond the zone of society. One of the Mahayana sutras says that taking seven steps toward the mountain has far more virtuous merit than making offerings of flowers and incense to all the buddhas for many eons. This is a very powerful analogy, especially for someone who grew up in a Buddhist culture. It points out the value and power of the inner stillness that comes from meditation. Here, the mountain can be regarded as the inner hermitage. This statement from the sutra also encourages people to find inner stillness, which is a vital part of their spiritual practice.

Experience of Happiness and Calmness

Many of the ancient Dzogchen masters fell in love with nature as a sanctuary, where they could drop into inner stillness and be free from the confinement of human society. They used nature, such as a forest, as an actual place to spend time as well as a metaphor for inner stillness. As Longchenpa wrote in his *Song of the Enchanting Forest*,

> No matter how much I reflect on it, there is no benefit [for being in the world].
> In order to become familiar with the enlightened view in one's mind,
> from today on, into the forest, you, dear mind—
> go there to seek ultimate happiness.

One often experiences pure joy or happiness simply from meditation practices. There are stories about people who spend time in solitude in the Himalayas practicing meditation, and they experience unbelievable levels of joy for no particular reason. This is because their mind breaks free from negative patterns as they immerse themselves in meditation without interruption from the outside world.

Shamatha Experiences

The reason pure joy emerges naturally as part of shamatha meditation is that our mind becomes completely peaceful when it is no longer dragged in all directions by our wild mental events. Whereas often in daily life, our mind is relentlessly bombarded by countless thoughts that create a general sense of being ill at ease. Even if we are not in any kind of real conflict and are in a relatively peaceful situation, there is still restlessness and lack of peace in our mind.

In shamatha meditation, our mind becomes still and calm, and many of our negative thoughts may not arise, or if they arise, they don't disturb our mind, since we are grounded in stillness. That state of peace comes with a sense of being happy, and that experience can be regarded as an indicator that shamatha is already developing in one's mind.

The calmness that comes from shamatha meditation has many positive effects. It helps us break free of our unhealthy mental patterns. It can help us reduce the level of stress and anxiety in daily life. I often call that calmness "the oasis within" or "the inner sanctuary." It is an oasis because we can always go there and find a sense of deep peace, even amid outer chaos that seems to be more and more part of our modern way of life.

The State of Stillness

It is said that it takes quite a while to achieve true shamatha, which is not just a temporary experience of being at peace but a state of the mind that is fundamentally changed and no longer bound by endless mental distraction. Such a state of stillness is called *shinjang* in Tibetan, which means "total flexibility." In this state, our mind becomes flexible, and we can direct it wherever we want it to go without needing to wrestle with it. We are no longer fighting with our mind.

Shinjang is a state of mind that is both flexible and still, accompanied by a sense of bliss. These experiences are described as attributes of shamatha in traditional scriptures and are also experienced by meditators who practice shamatha.

The Mind Has Its Own Mind

We don't know the exact percentage of the population without any type of meditation or inner reflection practice. But without such a practice, it is very easy for someone to live unconsciously, being ruled by old mental patterns and believing their thoughts. In that case, people may not even struggle or fight with their minds but go along with the dictates of their mind's view of reality.

Once we become more spiritual and begin to reflect inwardly, we don't suddenly gain control over our mind. Sometimes we go through a stage where we feel we have to fight and wrestle with our mind. It would be easier if our mind did everything we wanted. But that is not the case in reality. Even if we are spiritual practitioners, we often struggle with our mind and are not particularly happy with it. Thoughts and emotions arise that we don't want to have, yet sometimes we feel we are stuck in them and don't know how to get out. Many of us want to feel a positive state of mind, like peace, joy, love, or even transcendence. But it feels as though our mind has a very powerful tendency to go in the other direction.

This kind of internal wrestling is humorously shown in a popular country-western song, "My Mind's Got a Mind of Its Own."

As meditators, we might burst out laughing when we listen to it because it describes the internal struggle between our will and the wild tendency of the mind. It's somewhat funny to notice that the whole idea of meditation practice is not to get lost in our thoughts, yet while meditating, we can be lost for hours and hours in the mind's chatter. It's like being on a healthy eating regimen yet sitting on the couch eating junk food all day.

If you ask people the question, "Are you happy with your mind?" most people may not say yes. The problem is that we are stuck with our mind. If you don't like a place, you can pack up and move somewhere else and get a new address, or even move to another country and become a naturalized citizen there. If you don't like the people around you, you can stop interacting with them and find a new community. But you cannot run away or escape from your mind. Even if you hypothetically could go to another planet far from Earth, your mind would still be with you.

So we need to wake up and realize that it is much better to work with our mind and learn how to tame it so that we do not feel that our old familiar mental patterns have the upper hand. Instead, the mind begins to transform. We can feel that we and our mind are in harmony, walking the same path together.

Freedom from the Undercurrent of Thoughts

There are other important marks or parameters for the beginning of authentic shamatha experiences. One of them is not being lost in the "undercurrent of thoughts," where one thinks one is in a meditative state, yet there is a lot of subconscious mental chatter happening. One can be quite lost in that without knowing it.

These mental events are not coarse enough to recognize them when we experience them. This situation is often described in traditional teachings as "water flowing under a haystack." This analogy invokes the image that while you are sitting in front of a haystack, maybe water is flowing underneath it, but you cannot see that it is happening.

In the same way, even when we think we are in a meditative state and fully present, our mind could be lost in mental events that are so subtle that we don't recognize they are happening. This undercurrent of thoughts does not necessarily refer to all forms of thought, but specifically to thoughts that are unwholesome and can cause us suffering or bring down the level of our consciousness. When we become aware of the undercurrent, we experience true shamatha.

Staying Fully Present

The authentic meditative state of shamatha is also not simply mindless or totally blank, like "zoning out." If you ever find yourself in that state while meditating, it can feel like such solace that time can fly by. But don't think that is real meditation. Shamatha has the quality of the mind being fully present. While practicing shamatha, you are able to experience inner serenity; coarse thoughts subside, but you are fully present. Your mind is alert and aware; it is not blank. There is a deep sense of peace along with a sense of being fully present.

Traditionally, Buddhist teachers remind us that we can waste a lot of time practicing meditation when it is done incorrectly. They even have a term, "idiot meditation," which refers to a blank state mistaken for shamatha or awareness. It can also refer to the meditation of someone stubbornly practicing meditation even though he or she doesn't know how to meditate in accordance with traditional instructions. The great Dzogchen master Dza Patrul Rinpoche, from the nineteenth century, said,

> In this present time,
> there are some gurus and disciples,
> where the guru teaches incorrectly and the disciples
>   meditate incorrectly.
> So even though they meditate for seventy or eighty years,
> many of them haven't had meditative experience and insight.

Patrul Rinpoche was known for being critical and satirical, and he did not hold back from speaking honestly when he felt people needed to hear it. In today's world, we are exposed to an enormous volume of information on Buddhist meditation everywhere, including online, in books, magazines, and so on. Even with that, it is wise to learn how to meditate from a living teacher who is a well-seasoned meditator.

The True Purpose of Shamatha

While shamatha meditation brings about invaluable experiences, such as inner peace, that is not the whole picture. Traditionally, shamatha is used as a vessel for vipashyana meditation or other forms of meditation. This is because if our mind is everywhere and distracted by mental events, it becomes much more challenging to do further meditation practices such as vipashyana. When our mind is completely calm, there is an interior environment where we can engage with deep inquiry or simply drop into rigpa.

In the beginning, if our mind is lost in the stream of thoughts and driven by our habitual impulses, it is challenging to engage in any kind of deeper spiritual practice. Not only that, it is hard to make the best choices in our lives. Sometimes people ask for my advice when making a decision that involves moral issues, or when they are at a crossroads where the decision may have a long-term impact. I often try not to give any concrete answers, since I don't know what the right choice is for them.

I usually tell them, "You might like to take some time to meditate. Once you reach inner stillness—where you're not so caught up in all the thoughts, opinions, worries, and judgments—you'll be able to connect with your innate wisdom. From there, you may get an answer you can trust."

In the same way, when our mind is completely calm and no longer dragged in all directions by internal forces, it becomes ready to drop into its most profound state.

Union of Shamatha and Vipashyana

In the Buddhist tradition, some people just do shamatha practice for a long period and then begin vipashyana meditation as a separate practice. You can also practice both shamatha and vipashyana in one meditation session. For example, in the meditation retreats that I lead, each meditation session lasts forty-five minutes. I often instruct people to start with concentrating on the breath for five minutes or longer, which is shamatha. Then we let go of concentration and witness whatever arises in nonjudging awareness. I call this vipashyana or meditation on rigpa, depending on the context of the practice at any given time.

Shamatha Experiences

All the precise explanations of shamatha and vipashyana can be useful meditation models for some people. And yet, in the purest sense of Dzogchen, there isn't any separation between these two practices of shamatha and vipashyana. There is a point where shamatha and vipashyana are no longer two different meditation practices. In this state, one can experience rigpa in total stillness, and one's mind is not disturbed by thoughts and emotions.

If we simply drop into rigpa, then shamatha and vipashyana are both completely there. We should not get too dogmatic about drawing boundaries between shamatha and vipashyana. They can overlap. In this way, shamatha is not separate from vipashyana, nor vice versa. In that state, the duality between them is transcended. So while we can practice them separately, in the end we have to realize they can be one experience. This was stated by many great Dzogchen masters.

Beyond Labels

In the Dzogchen tradition, it is not always necessary to create a step-by-step relationship between shamatha and vipashyana where shamatha must precede vipashyana for a certain amount of time. The tranquility and insight aspects of our mind in meditation can be regarded as the union of shamatha and vipashyana.

The ultimate goal of Dzogchen meditation is to drop into rigpa. As we do that, all the qualities, such as tranquility and insight, emerge naturally without needing to apply the separate labels of shamatha and vipashyana. Ultimately, we have to transcend these labels and not be attached to them.

Practicing Dzogchen meditation is not about becoming a good meditator or a professional meditator, or turning meditation into a compulsion. It is all about remaining in rigpa, pure awareness, as much as possible. Every time we meditate, our mind becomes more and more united with rigpa, so we can integrate rigpa into our everyday life. Then at some point, we don't even have to call it meditation.

Abiding in Open Awareness

བདེ་གསལ་མི་རྟོག་ཉམས་ནི་གང་སྐྱེས་ཀྱང་། །
མི་ཆགས་མི་ཞེན་ཆེད་བསྒོམ་དོགས་སྤང་མེད། །
བདེ་ན་བདེ་མཁན་གསལ་ན་གསལ་མཁན་ཏེ། །
དོ་བོ་ཉིད་ལས་རང་བཞིན་སྤྱོད་འདོད་མེད། །
བདེ་མཁན་གསལ་མཁན་གནས་མཁན་དེ་ག་སྐྱོངས། །

Whatever experiences arise—be they bliss, clarity, or no-thought—
do not grasp, do not cling, do not deliberately meditate, and do not abandon due to fear.
When there is bliss, there is the experiencer of bliss; when there is clarity, there is the experiencer of clarity.
Apart from being in their essence, do not desire to engage with them as the nature [of mind].
Maintain that which is the experiencer of bliss or clarity, as it is.

6

Doorways to Awareness

Meditation is an amazing spiritual and psychological tool that can help us bring about inner peace, understand ourselves, and even experience a profound inner awakening. It is one of the best discoveries of humanity. It's almost impossible to figure out a single person or group who came up with meditation; it's like trying to find out who first discovered fire. Its essence is universal and transcends culture and religion. It is a practice that can benefit anyone, regardless of their way of life or background.

Meditation can be regarded as a gift of the mind to the mind itself. Even though the mind can create its own web and get trapped in it, it also has an innate and remarkable intelligence that can eventually figure out how to free itself—even after being tormented for a long time. The best remedy for all the mind's problems is meditation, which is an expression of the natural intelligence of the human mind. It is as if the mind finally figured out how to undo the self-trapping web it has been creating for ages.

Some ancient writings use the silkworm's activities as an analogy for the mind's tendency to bind itself. The silkworm creates thread from its saliva, then binds itself in its own cocoon. In the same way, the mind binds itself in the trap of concepts and ideas. From the Dzogchen point of view, often the mind's best efforts to free itself end up continuing the same problems, binding itself even more. Dzogchen meditation invites us to experience the nature of reality directly and not get trapped by anything whatsoever, including Buddhist doctrines and concepts.

Meditation Is Humanistic

Meditation is timeless, transcendental, and humanistic. It is a tool that allows us to actualize the best or even the highest capacity of our mind, which can benefit everyone.

Some people believe that society will never be enlightened, which sounds very pessimistic in many ways. I have no illusion that everyone in the world would be practicing meditation. But we should never rule out any possibilities. Wouldn't it be wonderful if society as a whole became enlightened, even if we can't picture what that would look like? It's always helpful to imagine positive possibilities for oneself and humanity. We could even write a new song called "Imagine," similar to John Lennon's version, with lyrics that describe a world where everyone meditated; there was no more war, aggression, violence, or greed; and everyone was kind toward each other.

No matter what it looks like on the outside, everyone does have an inner impulse for the well-being of society. No one ever wants a world filled with suffering, even though some political systems, as well as some religious practices, can sometimes be so flawed that it seems they cause more trouble to the world than benefit.

The very idea of meditation is not archaic but resonates with the ethos of modern times. In some sense, it is very humanistic because we use our inner capacity to change ourselves rather than rely on some higher force or external agent to redeem us.

Believe it or not, I think people are very evolved in today's world and are continually evolving for the better. There is, I feel, so much more compassion, greater tolerance, and a stronger sense of unity than perhaps ever before in human history. Even with the dynamic of two steps forward and one step backward, we are still moving forward. Meditation has the power to expedite humanity's evolution if there are enough people in the world who practice it.

A wonderful development is that Buddhist meditation is no longer for a select group of people, such as monastics. In today's world, many laypeople are learning and practicing meditation everywhere, transcending the old rules of social and gender differences about who can practice.

Flexibility of the Mind

The mind turns out to be flexible, even though that may seem contrary to our common experience. In general, many of us feel our mind's resistance to change is a formidable force that has the upper hand. It often takes a long time to see obvious evidence that our mind is transforming, even if we are meditation practitioners. Yet every now and then, the mind shocks us by its radical change simply by some obvious or mysterious catalyst.

There was a beloved lama from the Golok region of Eastern Tibet who lived in the twentieth century. He was considered a living bodhisattva, a saint who was loved by many. His nickname was Mani Lama because he traveled everywhere, inviting laypeople and monastics to recite the Mani mantra, the name of Avalokiteshvara. It was said that one time, when he was a young man, he was visiting a family who, at that same time, was hosting a lama. The lama started reciting a liturgy, and Mani Lama overheard one verse and had an epiphany that completely transformed his consciousness. This changed the course of his life forever. Some say that what he experienced was rigpa. This is one of many anecdotes that show that the mind can be completely transformed in an immediate and sudden fashion.

Even modern neuroscience is discovering the flexibility of our brain. It was once thought that when we reached a certain age, our neurological patterns were set and not easily changed. Now, neuroscientists are discovering that our brains can be rewired throughout our lives; they call this process "neuroplasticity." So it is never too late to attend to our mind and transform it. The moment our mind transforms, we feel our entire life and even the whole world transform because how we see the world lies "in the eye of the beholder."

Once, Rigdzin Jigme Lingpa was practicing meditation in a cave at Samye Chimpu, a place blessed by Padmasambhava and Yeshe Tsogyal. In one of his dohas, he describes how joyous he is because he has everything he needs; nothing is lacking. He even metaphorically describes his cave as a palace, the rock formations as furniture, and fire stones as his personal attendants. Obviously, Rigdzin Jigme Lingpa was not high from taking some pills; he was experiencing bliss from finding wonder in his simple environment because his mind was free from the usual neurotic patterns.

If our mind is not so stuck in its deep-seated patterns, it has extraordinary potential, allowing us to experience a world that is beautiful and sacred. Then we may be able to see ourselves and everyone else through another eye of consciousness.

Vipashyana Meditation

As we said earlier, even in Dzogchen, we can refer to two categories of meditative practices: shamatha and vipashyana. We have already discussed shamatha in detail.

Vipashyana is the main form of Buddhist meditation practiced in all Buddhist traditions. Yet the techniques and outer forms vary. In the West, people often associate vipashyana with the Theravadin tradition, partly because its practitioners tend to use that label for meditation, calling it by the Pali term, *vipassana*.

Vipashyana, which can be translated in various ways, means "direct seeing" into the nature of reality, or special insight. But the question is, what is to be seen? One could say that what is seen is the true nature of reality, which is transitory and lacking intrinsic solidity. Does that mean we don't usually see the nature of reality? In everyday life, we don't usually have an ounce of doubt that we are seeing reality. We are convinced that what we see and believe is reality. But we are not truly seeing reality as it is. Instead, we see a provisional reality that is constructed out of our thoughts, opinions, ideas, and so forth. From that point of view, our mind is often deluded, even though we don't think that about ourselves. Yet, this condition of delusion is the main factor for all the suffering and problems in this world. Vipashyana, in this context, is seeing reality as it is, not through the distortion of our thinking mind.

Rigpa and Pointing-Out Instructions

In Dzogchen, one could say that vipashyana is the direct seeing of the luminous, pristine nature of mind, or rigpa. This also indicates that our usual mind is veiled by all types of internal obscurations that prevent it from experiencing its own true nature—the very nature of mind itself.

Rigpa is not an altered state of mind. It is not an effect of any cause but rather the natural state of one's mind, the primordial dimension of one's mind prior to the thinking mind or ego development. This state of mind is also known as the pristine nature of mind, which has the connotation that it is pure, not conditioned by any human neurosis, and full of potential.

There are specific methods to make sure the meditator experiences rigpa in the most correct way. One of the methods is to receive *ngotröd*, which is a Tibetan word that means "pointing-out instructions." According to the Dzogchen tradition, this is considered the ultimate teaching that anyone can offer you in this human world.

Traditionally, you have to request ngotröd from a teacher; not just any teacher but an authoritative Dzogchen master who is revered and considered authentic. Even if you find a Dzogchen master and ask them for ngotröd, there is no guarantee they will fulfill your request right away. Sometimes, they may tell you that you are not ready for it. Other times, they may tell you that you are ready and will offer it.

Some of these Dzogchen masters are very intuitive, and they can see someone's readiness. This ability is more than just something you hear in orally circulating stories about ancient masters who lived hundreds of years ago. For example, the late Khenpo

Munsel from the twentieth century was said to be one such master. He was very kind and, at the same time, straightforward and stern. When people went to him to receive ngoträd or study Dzogchen, sometimes he would look at the person and say, "I won't be able to communicate with you," and he would send them away. Other times, he asked people to stay around, sometimes for months, before he would give them ngoträd. And now and then, he would give ngoträd right away to some people and then send them away, as if they had learned everything they needed from him.

Ngoträd is a nonconceptual and sometimes improvisational teaching. There are stories about Dzogchen masters who don't say much and simply sit with you during ngoträd. Or they may employ various spontaneous methods, like displaying sacred symbols, using hand gestures, saying a few words, or shouting a mantra. Yet when there is an openness in our consciousness, we can experience what ngoträd is trying to point out, which is rigpa, the pristine nature of our own mind, the sole goal of Dzogchen practice.

The Senses as a Doorway to Rigpa

This pristine dimension of mind is much bigger than having a meditative experience of being in the present moment and not being traumatized by one's own wild thoughts and emotions for half an hour. That being said, there are many methods that allow our mind to awaken to its pristine nature.

One of the most immediate ways to experience rigpa is by being fully present with your experiences, including all your senses, without labeling, judging, or naming. This can be too simple for many people and may not mean anything. They can say,

"Being present . . . so what?" But if you are lucky enough, before you know it, this is all that you need to land in the "rigpa zone."

Once, Patrul Rinpoche and Nyoshul Lungtok were in the hills above Dzogchen Monastery in Tibet. Nyoshul asked Patrul Rinpoche for ngotröd. Patrul Rinpoche was someone who was discreet about offering it. But one evening, he said he was ready to give ngotröd and asked Nyoshul to lie on his back and describe his experience.

Nyoshul said something like, "My last thought came to an end, my next thought hasn't arrived. Nothing is happening, but I hear the nomad's dogs barking in the distance, see the moon in the sky, feel the gentle wind brushing my skin."

Patrul Rinpoche said, "That's it. That's rigpa." That was the end of the pointing-out instruction.

Nyoshul experienced rigpa in that moment. Then later, he said, "It's very hard to describe. When I tell my experience, it sounds like I am saying that the eye consciousness, ear consciousness, and so forth are rigpa. But it's more than that."

Because he was ready, dropping into the senses allowed him to experience rigpa. For him, it was a doorway that worked. This is partly because when we simply drop into the pure senses and don't engage with the thinking mind, there is no longer a veil obscuring the pure nature of mind itself, which is free from the ego.

Even in this moment, while you are reading, just sit still. Don't block your senses; let your ears hear sound, your body feel touch, and your heart feel moods and emotions. Don't do anything; don't follow your experiences. Don't label anything that might arise in your senses. Let all your experiences arise purely as they are. The secret is not letting your thinking mind influence them by judging or labeling. Then it is possible to drop into a non-egoic, nonreactive, nonconceptual place that sees the pure dimension of mind, which is the true foundation of mind itself. It can be as simple as that.

Leaving the Senses Open

In Dzogchen, the idea of leaving the door of the senses open is very crucial in meditation. We simply witness whatever occurs in open awareness—all the rising and passing stimuli—and yet don't label or judge them. Instead, we welcome all of them as if they are the same. We welcome them with an all-embracing attitude, seeing them as self-arisen expressions of life or nature. They can even be regarded as the display of something ineffable. If we use Dzogchen language, we see them as "the display of rigpa."

To be in this state is not that difficult at all, but it is utterly radical because it is in juxtaposition with the state of our everyday mind, which is constantly judging, liking, disliking, labeling, and so forth. When the senses are completely pure without being distorted by our thinking mind, we are experiencing the pure nature of our mind as well as reality. As a Dzogchen tantra says,

> When the five sense consciousnesses are clear,
> if the mind's grasping and thinking do not enter,
> that very state is the realization of the buddhas.

The whole idea of just relaxing in open awareness of the senses may sound too simple. But this is the state of mind where we have an opportunity to experience the non-egoic, pure nature of our mind as well as life as it is.

The Open Secret of Mind

The experience of rigpa can sound like we are tapping into transcendence because it is a completely egoless state of consciousness where all our fear, greed, and attachment dissolve. Yet, when we experience it, it is profound and simultaneously simple and ordinary. We can call it a transcendent or sublime state of consciousness, but we are just returning to the fundamental nature of our consciousness. This is why Lama Mipham said, "The reason we don't realize the secret of mind is that it is so easy, we don't believe it."

So the doorway to transcendence can be much easier than we think. Dzogchen meditation is about experiencing transcendence in the realm of here and now, without needing to go somewhere or needing some powerful or auspicious circumstances, and especially without needing to do tricks to our mind.

Since rigpa is the original nature of our mind, it is always accessible to us. This is an experience that we can all witness. It is possible that now and then, we drop into that state of mind without even knowing it. Sometimes we may drop into it naturally, without any previous meditation training, and may even be able to recognize its profundity. I have run into many people who say they have had profound spiritual experiences on their own at an early age, and the description of what they experienced sounds very much like an experience of rigpa.

One time, Lama Garwang, one of my Dharma teachers, went to receive ngotröd from a well-known lama known as Kathok Khenpo Jampal Gyamsto. This lama agreed to give him ngotröd. Right after ngotröd was given, Lama Garwang said, "Is that all? I knew this all along since I was little." Lama Garwang's reply was not an expression of discontent but a humorous acknowledgment of his own experience. He had a profound inner awakening at an early age, even though he didn't call it that. This reminds us that we can experience rigpa in a spontaneous fashion in our life, even if we don't label it as rigpa.

There are spiritual lineages and spiritual practices that help us experience rigpa, but none of them own it. Rigpa is limitless like the sky and has no boundaries. Thinking that rigpa belongs to one tradition is a kind of delusion, like thinking that one owns the sky. Rigpa is a universal experience that can happen to anyone, and there is no gender or age limit either. It is all about returning to the deepest dimension of our consciousness.

Enlightenment as a Lived Experience

Rigpa, the pristine nature of mind, is a state of our consciousness that is more fundamental than any thoughts or emotions we are familiar with, even more fundamental than the unconscious aspects of our mind where all our habits live. Dzogchen teaches that rigpa is the primordial ground of mind because it is present in each of us all along. It exists prior to the development of the ego and all our mental conditioning. Whenever we are able to experience it, we are enlightened in that moment.

On the other hand, it is not as if we become someone else. We are simply returning to the primordial ground of our own consciousness. This invites us to understand enlightenment not as becoming something sublime but as returning to who we truly are—our original nature.

Sometimes the notion of awakening or enlightenment needs to be understood in context, since the meaning can vary from tradition to tradition and from individual to individual. There is a saying that goes,

> If you meditate on Dzogchen in the morning, you will be enlightened in the morning.
> If you meditate on Dzogchen in the evening, you will be enlightened in the evening.

This states that awakening, or enlightenment, can happen in an immediate fashion, which may sound implausible or illogical. According to Dzogchen, the logic behind that saying is that enlightenment is about reconnecting with the state of who we truly are; therefore, such spontaneous awakening is genuinely possible.

In contrast, many other Buddhist tenets may teach that enlightenment is some kind of achievement, where the mind is transformed into a sublime state rather than returned to its original nature. In that case, enlightenment is the result of a long process, an effect of a cause.

So the idea of enlightenment does not have any timeless, standard definition that everyone agrees on. This has been true even within Buddhist traditions throughout history. When we have too precise a definition of enlightenment, it tends to become dogmatic: we develop an "enlightenment scale" in our heads and try to squeeze all experiences into it. If the experience doesn't fit, we say it's not enlightenment, and if it fits, we say it is. This can lead to sectarianism, where we believe only people in our tradition can become enlightened, and we easily discard the profound experiences of people from different traditions. We think we have the correct scale, and no one else does.

Not only that, this can become a personal obstacle because we may fail to value our own profound spiritual experiences. In our mind, they might not fit into some lofty, mental category of enlightenment. This is not by any means encouraging us to take enlightenment lightly or to easily claim to others that we have had an enlightenment experience. On the other hand, we often come across powerful and profound experiences that we don't always categorize as some kind of spiritual experience, such as rigpa, awakening, or satori. But those experiences can be moments when we are in touch with transcendence and should be valued.

From time to time, we step out of the pigeonhole of our regular state of consciousness to witness something greater than ourselves, where we feel we are part of something truly indescribable. The experience comes with a feeling of awe and being deeply moved.

This doesn't belong exclusively to the territory of religion. Even people who identify themselves as secular speak about tapping into such experiences, which they may sometimes call "spiritual." These experiences can sometimes be triggered by being in nature, happen spontaneously, or arise even through suffering. They can have a positive impact on the rest of one's life.

The Three Immovables

Even though there is a possibility that we can drop into rigpa in the most immediate and direct way without relying on techniques, Dzogchen offers a form that can be very conducive to dropping into this state. It is called the three immovables (in Tibetan, *mi yo wa sum*): *immovable body*, *immovable senses*, and *immovable nature of mind*. This is one of the more convenient meditation forms among all others. The analogies used for these three immovables are:

> Immovable body is like Mount Meru;
> Immovable senses are like stars reflected in a lake;
> Immovable nature of mind is like a cloudless sky.

Immovable Body

The first immovable is the body. Immovable body means you sit in the meditation posture that we described in a previous chapter. You simply relax in that posture without movement until the meditation session ends. If you are moving around, it can change and interrupt the auspicious posture designed to create an energetic vessel in your being that allows you to drop into awareness. The power of this posture is supported by Tantric Buddhist science. A famous saying goes like this:

> If the body is straight, then the channels are straight.
> If the channels are straight, then the *prana* is straight.
> If the prana is straight, then the mind is flexible.

Sometimes Tantric Buddhism uses the analogy that the body is like a city, the channels are like the roads, the prana (vital force) is like a horse, and the mind is the rider. This shows that these psychobiological elements have a symbiotic relationship with each other, such that one element can influence the others.

We also see this in daily life when we are more aware of our body and mind. If we sit in a certain posture, it changes our mood and even our experience of ourselves. Other people around you also feel the power of your presence.

The meditation posture is a well-proven, perfect psychobiological environment where we can easily drop into rigpa. Therefore, relaxing in it for a certain period without wavering will help us experience rigpa and remain in that state effortlessly.

The analogy of Mount Meru, considered the queen of all mountains, represents dignity, stillness, and a sense of being unshakable. In the collective imagination, mountains generally represent these qualities. Invoking this analogy can help people feel the energetic qualities of the posture, such as stillness and groundedness.

Immovable Senses

The second immovable is immovable senses, often described as the stars and moon reflected in a lake. It indicates that the senses are not shut down but are completely loose and free, allowing everything to arise clearly through the doors of the senses.

This allows you to feel you are abiding in a spacious, open awareness where all experiences and stimuli are welcome—sights, sounds, touch, taste, and smell. Without judging or labeling them, and without holding on to any of them, you let them arise and disappear on their own.

Sometimes in the context of Dzogchen meditation, we are encouraged to open our eyes but not move them around too much. The purpose of this is to be in open, spacious awareness, not narrowing one's concentration on a particular object or drawing the attention inward and blocking the senses. This sitting posture is, in fact, the opposite of sensory deprivation. However, moving your eyes around will lead to wavering from awareness. So even if your eyes are open, it is important to keep them still.

In the modern world, many people meditate with their eyes closed. I feel you can meditate in rigpa with your eyes closed as long as you are not blocking your senses—you can still hear sounds and feel sensations. The point is not just about physically leaving the eyes open or not; it is about leaving the senses open. Then, as sensory stimuli arise, just don't follow them. Let them arise freely, without trying to avoid them or engage with them.

It is important not to get too hung up on these techniques. They are helpful tips that you can use. You can meditate perfectly without being too rigid about them. So . . . chill out!

Immovable Nature of Mind

The third immovable is immovable nature of mind. The analogy for this is a cloudless sky. The cloudless sky indicates that awareness is spacious, open, fully present, alert, and not bombarded with ordinary thoughts and emotions.

When we sit in these postures with the senses completely open and don't engage with our experiences while welcoming them, we can naturally drop into rigpa. This experience has two qualities: stability and clarity. The first, stability, means that the mind is no longer wandering. It is completely present with a sense of calmness and stillness. Clarity means that one's awareness is more than just still; it is also wide open, experiencing the sensory phenomena.

In this context, Dzogchen masters often invite us to put more emphasis on the clarity aspect rather than on calmness and stability. They state that spending too much time on stability and stillness would not lead to authentic awakening. Not only that, our meditation could fall into a cozy, unconscious state of mind, which could be regarded as mundane meditation. Attending to the clarity aspect can lead to a powerful spiritual awakening, including creativity, insight, and love. In other words, our consciousness will expand.

Transitory Meditation Experiences

As we continue to practice meditation, especially in a retreat setting for a long period, our mind will naturally go through a series of transformations. Most of them can be so pleasant and positive that we may regard them as spiritual attainments or enlightenment. Many of the transformative experiences are to be welcomed and are indicators that a crack is happening in our consciousness, as if it is ready to shed its limiting shell of habits. We don't have to try to produce them, as they will arise naturally.

Of course, these *nyam*, or "spiritual experiences," are very personal and cannot be categorized easily. And yet, there are three kinds of nyam that Dzogchen meditators often come across: bliss, clarity, and no-thought. These three experiences can arise any time during meditation. One can experience them while practicing shamatha or open awareness. Traditionally, they have been mapped out precisely, and their idiosyncrasies are described in many Dzogchen texts.

Bliss does not just refer to some kind of pleasure that comes from the senses; rather it is a deep, profound joy where all sense of suffering is completely dissolved. Clarity is when the mind is totally alert, pristine, and there is not an iota of a sense of dullness or sleepiness, yet we are fully present. No-thought is when all mental activities have subsided, and our consciousness feels as expansive as the sky.

These experiences are regarded as a sign of progress, yet they can be very addictive. Not only that, meditators may easily think that these are the goal and may practice meditation just to produce those experiences. Being attached to them becomes an obstacle because they are not the state of rigpa. They are transitory, wonderful experiences, similar to beautiful experiences in daily life, like the magical experience of watching the sunset. So when they arise naturally, we can enjoy them without grasping or reifying them.

Gyedro Wonpo was a twentieth-century, dynamic, and skilled Dzogchen master from the Golok region of Tibet. He was known for not letting students get attached to *nyam* and for keeping them very grounded. One time, one of his students, a monk who was practicing Dzogchen with him, reported his experience. "I started seeing rainbows everywhere," the monk said. Gyedro Wonpo, instead of validating and praising this experience, replied, "Perhaps you had a stroke."

Another time, a nun told him that she was having amazing visions in her meditation practice, where she felt she had become a vulture, flying with other vultures to visit charnel grounds. She said, "I feel I am a dakini," who are considered "sky dancers." Dakinis are Tantric Buddhist female deities, and some Tibetans believe that some vultures are emanations of dakinis. Gyedro Wonpo drolly replied, "Well, maybe it's a sign you are going to die very soon."

This does not mean that Gyedro Wonpo was ruthless or disrespectful, but he may have known that these students were becoming attached to their experiences and creating stories about them. He saw that this would become an obstacle for their Dzogchen practice, so he made these seemingly unappreciative statements in reply to encourage them to let go of their fixation on nyam.

Breaking Identification with Experiences

So, now and then, we might want to check whether we are attached to nyam, believing they are the true meditation that we want to prolong. If you feel you are attached to the experiences, thinking, "I'm achieving the true meditation now," you might let go of the whole idea that you're doing this thing called "meditation." This is what Padmasambhava's words refer to when he said,

> Although many know how to build up meditation,
> no one knows how to dismantle meditation better than I do.

We should bear in mind that the objective of Dzogchen meditation practice is not to journey into some wonderful state of mind but to truly change ourselves as a person from the inside. This requires changing our consciousness so that we are able to integrate the wisdom of meditation with everyday life. Not only will we be happier and wiser as individuals, but we will be able to deal with all types of situations from a more enlightened state of mind. We won't be thrown off-balance or be at the mercy of our internal neurotic patterns, which are easily triggered by the smallest discomfort from outside.

If we get attached to these meditative experiences, we can look into them and see who is experiencing them. We usually discover that mind alone is the one who is the experiencer.

With that recognition, we don't need to do anything further. We don't have to change, alter, or modify the mind. That recognition can immediately help us to continuously witness all the meditative experiences yet not get hooked by them.

Every now and then, if we feel we are stuck with nyam or even with thoughts, we might like to apply some methods to shake the identification with the experience. One popular traditional method is the exclamation of the mantric syllable PHAD (sometimes pronounced like "putt"). It can be just pure sound, or it can have all sorts of significance. Traditionally, Dzogchen masters encourage us to shout "PHAD" so loudly that it has a shocking impact on our system, disrupting our attachment to experiences.

One time, I was leading a retreat in Northern California and told people that if they were lost in their thoughts, they should just shout "PHAD." I sent everyone to meditate outdoors. During a break, a person approached me and said, "I was so lost in thoughts that I had to repeat "PHAD" all the time. I felt I had become like a tractor, going 'Putt, Putt, Putt . . .'"

Non-Meditation Meditation

In general, we human beings are very interested in exploring our consciousness and mind. There is a sense that there is a new frontier in our own consciousness. People may use different means or techniques to discover it, including spiritual practices as well as other things, such as substances. Often, people think that the frontier of our mind and consciousness is an ecstatic, expansive, and even insightful state, quite apart from the ordinary mind. But in truth, the furthest frontier of our consciousness is already here. Without using substances or fancy spiritual practices, we can discover the most profound and deepest terrain of our consciousness by not doing anything.

So sometimes Dzogchen uses a paradoxical term, *meditation without meditation*. This can be confusing to many people, especially if they are not familiar with such concepts.

The whole premise of Dzogchen is that the nature of mind is already enlightened. This is what it means to say the nature of mind is luminous. This is a fundamental doctrine of not just Dzogchen but all Mahayana. But it seems that Dzogchen has a powerful way to lead us to experience it in the realm of here and now rather than treating it as a philosophical matter.

It makes a huge difference when we think of meditation as a practice that would alter our mind versus thinking of meditation as a way to drop into the natural state of our mind as it is. The former is about modifying the mind to get into a specific state. The latter is not about modifying our state of mind but rather returning to the purest state of our mind as it is.

In the true sense, therefore, Dzogchen meditation is not even meditation. Dzogchen meditation is about dropping into the very natural state of mind as it is.

Letting Go of Activities and Concepts

Sometimes in a Dzogchen retreat, the practice becomes utterly simple, so simple that there is not much to do either physically or mentally. There is a particular practice called "letting go of the ninefold activities," referring to the activities of body, speech, and mind. In essence, it is about dropping all our activities—not just ordinary ones, but even the spiritual ones—and simply resting in awareness. This does not mean that we literally should do that for the rest of our lives—that may be impossible. And it definitely doesn't mean we should drop all other spiritual practices forever. It is simply to enter a period now and then—for example, a certain time of day, or a weeklong or monthlong meditation retreat—where we apply this unassuming yet very powerful practice of letting go of all activity and resting completely. It is harder than you think!

So while we are meditating, we may need to let go of the concept of "I'm meditating" along with every other idea of what we are doing. In that nondoing state, there is a point where even the identity of the meditator dissolves. The very sense of "I" who is the meditator—who is striving and making sure to do this thing called "meditation" correctly—dissolves. There is no longer an "I" that is a separate entity from the rest of the world, so much so that the sense of the boundary between self and others, outside and inside, dissolves. The egoic self that we have been identifying as the basis of our identity goes away as if it never existed. Yet we are not completely gone. We are fully present with whatever is happening. The one who is witnessing being alive in that moment is not the ego but awareness itself.

7

Dzogchen Inquiry

Dudjom Lingpa taught that all apparent existence is a display of the mind itself. This principle is not just Dudjom Lingpa's wisdom but is also the essential doctrine of Dzogchen. It is the notion that things are not as real as they appear to us. The "realness" of everything we are experiencing, including the mind itself, is fundamentally a construction of our mind.

This is not just a lofty theory—it is a wisdom that we can bring into life and live by. It is also much more aligned with the true nature of reality than what our mind perceives every day. When we are able to truly embody and live this wisdom, we feel liberated because we see that many of the conflicts in our lives, as well as the fundamental sense of self, are not intrinsically real. They are just a powerful play happening in the theater of our mind.

Those who lived with such wisdom are considered mahasiddhas according to Tibetan culture. Dudjom Lingpa was a true mahasiddha who was a living testimony to this wisdom, embodying it in his life. He has been described as someone who was fearless. Often, our fear comes into being when we believe that the self, the problems, and the struggles in our lives have intrinsic existence. When someone truly realizes that they are all just big stories in their own mind, they become liberated and fearless. When our consciousness is not frozen by fear, then love, joy, and compassion shine naturally, just as the sun shines when it is no longer veiled by the clouds.

There is an inquiry in Buddhism that leads us to the understanding that the way we experience everything is merely the mind entertaining itself with its own mental constructs. The power of this analytical method is summarized by the phrase, "nothing stands in the face of inquiry." It means that there is nothing that really is solid when we inquire into its true nature; everything collapses as if it has been an illusion all along.

This method of inquiry is an uncompromising invitation to a daring adventure into the secret of all phenomena. We are invited to inquire not just into mundane things but also into things that we worship and revere as the highest, as the sacred. Basically, everything we believe to be true collapses right there in the face of such deep inquiry, like a house of cards.

One time, I was leading a weekend retreat in Southern California and talking about this inquiry. During a break, a woman approached me and said, "This sounds like a phrase from *Alice in Wonderland*. Alice looked at the Queen of Hearts and said, 'You're all nothing but a pack of cards!' At that moment, the Queen and her court of playing cards collapsed."

I think this is a wonderful analogy for the power of inquiry.

Dzogchen Inquiry

"Who Am I?"

It may not be challenging for us to inquire into something we are not particularly attached to because it is not a big deal to us whether it is real or not. But if something is especially dear to us, it might be too challenging to even question whether it is real or not. Perhaps what is most dear to us is our very identity. There are some radical ways to let go of that identity. It is said that some creative Dzogchen masters sent their students into the mountains, wandering along the riverbanks, to look for themselves by calling their own name out loud.

At first, you may not take this whole thing too seriously if someone asks you to do this. But if you end up doing this inquiry, make sure you are alone, as it could be spooky for people to see you walking around, calling your own name. They might think you are losing it.

Imagine your name is Joe, and you walk around calling "Joe!" You could even spook yourself in the beginning, but it could have the power to shake the very idea of who you are in your mind. Once you get into the deeper inquiry of who you are, you may see that every iota of your identity is the mind's invention and is found neither outside nor inside.

I think I am Anam Thubten, yet even that is not true in an ultimate sense. If I look deeply, there's no Anam Thubten. People call me Anam Thubten all the time, and I believe I truly am Anam Thubten. In my mind, it is already well established and out of the question that I am not. But I wasn't born with this name. Anam means "Big Sky" in Tibetan. Thubten was the name given by my abbot when I was ordained as a monk, and I still carry that name, even though later I became a layperson. Thubten means *buddha-shasana*, or "Buddha Dharma."

When you become a monk, you always receive a new name, and all the names are fancy. They never give you a bad name. When you become a monk, they give you names like "Ocean of Dharma," "Lamp of the Buddha," "Light of the Dharma," and so forth. They never give inauspicious names like "Ocean of Stupidity" or "Castle of Hatred." All the names that they give are really good.

The truth is that Anam Thubten is a persona that society and I created. It is purely a mental construct, and there is no truth in that identity whatsoever.

Then who am I? Most probably, we may think, "My name and role in society are mental constructs, but at least I'm a person."

But what does "person" actually mean? If we keep inquiring, then we may feel that we are just a whirling bundle of particles governed by the laws of physics. If we continue to inquire, then what is a particle? What is physics?

And who is even perceiving all of this? This is similar to the Dzogchen inquiry of trying to find the self in our body and not finding anything that we can point to as the self.

Then we may come to the realization that all reality is just a display of our consciousness, and we may feel that consciousness is real. It is the last thing that we can hold on to to soothe ourselves from the terror of existential collapse.

But Dzogchen doesn't let us indulge in this delusional comfort of having something to latch on to, like an ontological pacifier. Traditionally, as part of Dzogchen training, we are invited to inquire into the existential nature of the mind and consciousness itself.

No Ground, No Root

Such inquiry reveals that the basis of our mind is not something we can find. This leads us to the ungraspable realization that the mind is neither existent nor nonexistent. It leads to a profound experience of the real nature of mind, known in Dzogchen as "no ground and no root." This is a state where the mind cannot be found anywhere; the mind is not a thing that has any location, any concreteness, or any particular idiosyncrasies.

There is a caution here—this inquiry does not lead us into a nihilistic negation of the mind. If the mind were completely nonexistent, we would not be experiencing anything.

As Jigme Lingpa said,

> It is not existent, because Buddha hasn't seen it.
> It is not nonexistent; it is the ground of all samsara and nirvana.
> It is not contradictory but is beyond words.

In this verse, Jigme Lingpa is stating that "not-finding" from such inquiry is not a road to the valley of existential death but a profound understanding of reality. We should all keep this wisdom in mind to ensure that our inner streak of nihilism doesn't take over.

What we call life—including the past, the future, the sense of self, and one's relationship to everyone else in the world—would not come into being if there were no mind. Without the mind, we wouldn't be able to feel that we are alive, enjoy the senses, be happy or brokenhearted, or find meaning in our lives. This is why the mind is an extremely important factor in our existence.

When someone dies, the body is no longer alive. It is simply an inanimate object, like a stone or a table. The body itself has no sense of being alive without the mind. In modern culture, when someone dies, people put nice clothes on the body and even makeup, so that when you look at the body, you feel it is the person you knew. But it is only in our mind that we perceive the body as a person. The body has no sense of self because consciousness left that body at death. This is just simple logic to illustrate that there is no life without the mind.

But our mind is extremely creative. It not only has the ability to experience the senses, such as taste, touch, and so forth, it also has the ability to construct stories. Sometimes the mind is like a creative writer, as if our life is fiction. Often, our mind forgets that it is simply writing fiction and starts believing the stories that it is manufacturing. Much of our human suffering comes from unfounded stories that the mind simply creates.

Even the sense of self is a creation of our mind. This truth is difficult to believe. It challenges the very idea of who we are, which is well established in our mind. But in profound inquiry, even this deeply held notion of self collapses. Then the separation between self and other also naturally goes away. Then you see the pure nature of reality where all the mental constructs—self and other, good and bad, past and future, here and there—dissolve. It is not that we can live in that state all the time, but with that experience, our fundamental way of looking at reality changes. This results in a freedom that cannot be obtained from anything outside.

In addition, the mind itself is not something we can hold on to. Inquiring into the nature of the mind is like going to the root of everything, both suffering and happiness. Dzogchen teaches that whenever the nature of mind is realized, that is the highest liberation, where we can be free from the snares of suffering that the mind creates for itself.

The nature of mind as "no ground, no root" uses the language of negation. There are also positive names and images that represent the nature of mind, such as dharmakaya mind. Dharmakaya is the highest level of enlightenment in Mahayana Buddhism, the most sacred of the sacred.

Inquiry into the Mind

The true nature of mind can be experienced by an inquiry that is taught very precisely in the Dzogchen tradition. Usually, it is done in a formal setting like a meditation retreat, where you take time away from your daily life and work on the inquiry without other distractions until an authentic insight shines forth.

The inquiry can begin with the same meditation posture that we already described. Then we may turn our attention to the mind itself intuitively and search for the mind by asking these three questions:

Where does it come from? Where does it reside? Where does it go?

Each one can be elaborated: Does it come from outside oneself, from within, or from different parts of the body?

Does it reside outside, inside, or in different parts of the body or organs? See if it is located there.

We can ask the same questions about where the mind goes.

We can elaborate on this inquiry by looking for the color, shape, and size of the mind.

Finally, we will come to the powerful conclusion that there is not one single phenomenon that is the mind. There is no "thing." Then the very foundation of the mind collapses in that state of not-finding, or "no ground, no root."

At the same time, as we already said, the mind is not totally nonexistent, or we wouldn't be experiencing anything. Yet arriving at the state of not-finding helps us let go of our grasping to our perceived reality and many of our painful, contracted experiences and thought patterns. Once we realize the mind is empty of solid existence, letting go of grasping at experiences becomes natural.

This state of not-finding may not sound inspiring because it is a negation, but through that, the egoic self and the contracted sense of reality can collapse on their own, just like the Queen of Hearts in *Alice in Wonderland*. This is because the mind is always sustaining them, so when the mind collapses, they all collapse too.

Inquiry from the Heart

Inquiry is taught in Buddhism in general and not just in Dzogchen. It has the power to shake the edifice of our old reality and lead to the collapse of our mind-manufactured illusions that cause so much suffering. However, many of the inquiries do not bring any real change in our consciousness if we practice them purely from our head. There is even a danger of getting lost in them, so inquiry becomes another form of intellectual entertainment.

The way for these inquiries to impact our inner life is to learn to practice them from our heart. Dzogchen, unlike many other Buddhist doctrines, emphasizes the development of devotion. Such devotion can be brought about by using various catalysts, including one's lineage gurus or the lineage itself. Therefore, guru yoga is used in Dzogchen as an indispensable foundation for our practice.

Devotion is like falling in love with the sacred. Devotion is nonconceptual. It is the authentic experience of your heart disarming itself. It takes us from the head into the heart. We become sincere and let go of all our intellectual games. Our heart has the willingness to let go of all forms of resistance in order to be free. That's what devotion is. Then finally, we learn how to engage in these inquiries from the most sincere and pure place in our heart, with an authentic desire to wake up. That makes all the difference. Once we know how to give rise to devotion, then all the practices work for us. They become extremely powerful, too.

When you think of some of the inspiring Dzogchen yogis and yoginis of the past, there is one thing common to all of them: they all had a powerful, unflinching devotion toward their gurus and their spiritual lineage. Yeshe Tsogyal's devotion to Padmasambhava and Anam Chatralwa's devotion to Dudjom Lingpa are just two of many examples. Such devotion was the most powerful force in their spiritual awakening.

Dzogchen master Adzom Drukpa studied under many contemporary Dzogchen masters, such as Patrul Rinpoche. Yet he said, "Even though all of my human gurus are very kind, the kindest one is Rigdzin Jigme Lingpa." This was an interesting statement because they lived centuries apart. It is said that, one time, Adzom Drukpa had a vision of Jigme Lingpa, who was laughing hysterically so loudly that Adzom Drukpa fainted. When he came to, he realized he had lost all sense of duality and any craving for further doctrines and teachings. This awakening came from the beautiful combination of his practice and his devotion to the lineage.

This type of anecdote is very common in the Dzogchen lineage, showing that devotion plays a key role in one's awakening. Without devotion, we can practice all the Buddhist inquiries, but they will not help us change our consciousness at a fundamental level.

Experiential, Not Intellectual

Dzogchen inquiry is not something we do for the rest of our lives. Once we come to the realization of "no ground, no root," we can simply practice formless meditation, dropping into the natural state of mind. However, such realization must be experiential rather than merely intellectual, and it must become part of our lived reality. It is something we understand both cerebrally and viscerally, so that there is no longer any question about it in our mind.

People often make the mistake of believing that intellectual understanding is sufficient. But the limitation of intellectual understanding is that it doesn't usually translate into our lived experience.

Naropa, one of the eighty-four Tantric Buddhist mahasiddhas from ancient India, was a great scholar who played an important role at Nalanda University. According to his biography, one day he had an encounter with a very wise woman, and they had a dialogue. She pointed out that he only had intellectual knowledge and not the real experience. This caused him to make a sudden decision to give up his studies and his role at Nalanda and to run away as a wandering mendicant. He eventually came across Tilopa, who turned out to be enlightened but was disguised as an ordinary layperson, a fisherman. By spending time with Tilopa, Naropa was able to go beyond the boundaries of intellectual knowledge and experience true awakening.

There are numerous stories about people who had incredible intellectual understanding but at some point, they realized that it was not the real thing. That realization became a turning point in their lives, ultimately leading them to authentic awakening.

If we are able to integrate the wisdom of our inquiry into our experience, there is no question that we will be truly free inside and able to embody love and compassion in everyday life. So the power of such inquiry is truly beyond measure.

In the old days, well-seasoned meditators would work with these inquiries wholeheartedly until they reached an experiential understanding of the radical truth about the mind. They didn't become content with just a cerebral understanding but had a direct experience of it and translated that experience into their lives. They lived as free or even spiritually awakened beings. I refer to them with a term of endearment: "holy happy campers." I have run into a few of them in my lifetime. These happy campers are not mythical; they are real, and they exist. It is so refreshing and inspiring to remember them and realize that they are real people. It gives me hope and aspiration that we can reach that state. To me, the term "happy camper" means that someone is easygoing, uncomplicated, fundamentally happy, and not tormented by cynicism, pessimism, or neurotic inner demons. In the end, that's all we need to become.

8

Meditation Guidance

In general, Dzogchen meditation is primarily about not altering the mind during meditation but instead leaving the mind as it is. From that point of view, whatever the mind is going through—whether meditative "highs" or just usual mundane experiences—it should be regarded as the perfect condition for meditation practice.

Therefore, theoretically, we can enter rigpa at any given moment because our mind doesn't have to be modified in any way. In one of his writings, Patrul Rinpoche answered the grievances of some meditators who felt it was difficult to recognize the essence of the mind. He said,

> There's no need to search for meditation. No need to buy it. No need to accomplish it. No need to go anywhere. No need to do anything. Simply rest in whatever arises and appears in your own mind. That alone is sufficient. Your own mind has been there from the very beginning. It is not

something that can be lost and then found. It is not something you have and then do not have.

The mind you have always had is what thinks when you are thinking, and rests without thoughts when you are not thinking. This very presence of awareness is who you are. Whatever arises in your own mind, just leave it as it arises, without fabrication, relaxing, and without distraction—that is enough. It will come naturally and easily, effortlessly.

As Patrul Rinpoche said, Dzogchen meditation is about settling or relaxing in whatever the mind experiences, without trying to modify anything. This can sometimes be counterintuitive. In the back of our mind, we may think we should change or manipulate our mind or present experiences whenever we meditate.

Sometimes, we may hold the belief that meditation is some kind of altered state of mind. Yet simply relaxing in whatever is happening and not trying to do anything with our mind brings a freedom where we are no longer rejecting or holding on to anything, and that itself is inner liberation. There is unfathomable peace and freedom in that state, and we are able to touch the more transcendent ground of our consciousness, where the ego is dissolved along with all its neurotic patterns.

Therefore, whether you are having powerful meditation experiences or ordinary thoughts, there is no need to change any of them. Just leave your mind alone as it is. Everything else is taken care of. You don't have to be the doer—you are off the hook! Don't go after anything, even spiritual awakening or enlightenment. Let them come to you. Just the way the sun rises—you cannot make the sun rise. But if you sit and wait, the sun shines by itself.

Meditation Guidance

Ordinary Mind

Dzogchen masters use different epithets for rigpa. Some of them are very elevated and sublime, and others are very down-to-earth. For example, there is a Tibetan phrase *tamal gyi shepa*, which literally means "ordinary mind."

Here, "ordinary" does not have a negative connotation, such as inferior. It means "as it is" right now. This connotes that the nature of the mind, without needing any transformation, is already liberated and free from all *klesha*s, or negative mental conditioning. It is the true buddha mind that resides in us all the time.

Often, there is so much confusion about the phrase "ordinary mind." This is not a new phenomenon; it was the case even in old Tibet. One possible mistake that arises is the misunderstanding that one can just be lost in egoic thoughts, thinking that the egoic mind is the enlightened mind. Another mistake is that the phrase becomes so elevated, such as "dharmakaya mind" and others, that it prevents us from experiencing rigpa right now, without doing anything to our mind.

In addition, this notion of ordinary mind can be so philosophical that sometimes we can miss the point. For example, in the Mahamudra tradition, the masters identified three kinds of ordinary mind, indicating that only the third one is the true "tamal gyi shepa." Perhaps these kinds of philosophical discussions came from the concern that people might get lost in ordinary thoughts while meditating. But I don't think any meditation teacher has ever said, "Now you can get lost in your thoughts."

Even though it sounds simple, "ordinary mind" is such a rich and powerful epithet for rigpa. It is really saying that the nature of *this* mind is already rigpa. One doesn't need to seek rigpa outside of the realm of *this* mind.

The phrase "tamal gyi shepa" is often used in Dzogchen meditation instructions. Some teachers invite us to meditate by saying something like this:

> Don't do anything with your mind. Leave your mind alone as it is right now. Let all the thoughts and emotions rise on their own. If you simply stay in nonjudging awareness, all of them will liberate on their own, and none of them will bind you. This is how to meditate on ordinary mind.

Sometimes during pointing-out instructions or meditation guidance, teachers add one more term, *daté*, which means "this, right now." They would say *daté tamal gyi shepa*, "this ordinary mind, right now." Sometimes, during the pointing-out instruction, the Dzogchen master may do something totally improvisational, like shouting "PHAD." At that moment, one loses all thoughts, but there is a sense of being fully alive and present. Then the master would say, "This present, ordinary mind is rigpa, as it is." If a student is ready, they are able to recognize the unconditioned nature of mind in that moment.

At other times, the direct realization of rigpa arises simply by being present and not following one's experiences, not trying to add or subtract anything from them. One doesn't think, "Now I have to experience ordinary mind, rigpa," and then try to elevate or manipulate what is happening.

Remember, the secret is "don't do anything to your mind." Leave your mind alone in its natural state, because the nature of mind is already enlightened. If you are ready, you can experience this simple yet extraordinary state of your mind in an ordinary fashion, right now, in this very moment.

Mind the Gap

I had a friend who was an American Buddhist nun and used to come to my retreats. Every now and then, I invited her to give a talk at the retreat. She often talked about the power of creating a space between thoughts. She would imitate a British accent and say, "Mind the gap," explaining that when you ride the London Tube, there is always an announcement at each train station to mind the gap between the train and the platform. Her analogy gave me a sense that being in awareness is not so difficult after all.

Sometimes Dzogchen masters also invite us to find a moment where the last thought has ended and the next thought hasn't yet arrived. Karma Lingpa was a renowned *terton*, or "treasure revealer," from the fourteenth century. In one of his teachings, he offered this clear instruction:

> Upon the vanishing of past thoughts without a trace
> and future thoughts are unarisen and fresh;
> in the present moment, when resting in the uncontrived,
>   natural state,
> in the ordinary mind of this present moment,
> when the mind looks directly at itself,
> there is nothing to be seen through looking—it is vividly
>   clear.
> Rigpa is vividly, nakedly clear.

In other words, Dzogchen masters say that the state of mind between thoughts, which is fully aware, vivid, and yet not mindless, is rigpa. This is helpful for beginning meditators because, in that moment, there is no stream of thoughts and emotions popping up. Because of that, we can experience the state of mind that is free from ego, attachment to the past, fear of the future, and so on. They are all gone in that moment. That gap is an immediate and powerful doorway to glimpse the state of mind that is so subtle, ordinary, and amazing.

Basically, you are there, alive, breathing. You haven't spent years and years to arrive at the pinnacle of spiritual practice. You have not become some holy being. Instead, as an ordinary human being, you have a chance to experience inner freedom where your true mind is completely unveiled, without being covered by all its conditioning. This experience can result in a profound epiphany where you recognize that all your usual neurotic thoughts and emotions are not the true nature of your mind. You see the possibility of experiencing a state of mind where neurotic mental events are no longer running the show.

Rest in the Experiencer

Some thoughts may hook you, and the more you watch them, the stronger they may become. But if you just say, "I'm not going to bother with them," and let the thoughts proliferate, sooner or later, they simply dissolve on their own since you are no longer fueling them. In other words, there's not even an effort to be a witness or "be in awareness"—just do nothing. Let the mind do whatever it does. The main thing is not to engage with it.

This is what Dudjom Lingpa is teaching. He said, "Maintain that which is the experiencer of bliss or clarity, as it is." This means we don't need to get rid of anything, whether bliss, nyam, or even ordinary thoughts. Don't try to transcend them. Let them be; let them continue. There is nothing to do except not identify with them. The moment you don't follow thoughts, your mind is already liberated from them, regardless of whether they continue or dissolve immediately.

Rigpa as the Natural State

Rigpa is the most natural state of our mind. There is nothing manufactured or contrived about it. Therefore, when we are in rigpa, we don't even have to intentionally make an effort to be in that state. When we don't do anything, when we don't follow our thoughts, sometimes right away, the mind drops into its pure, original nature.

There is a term in Dzogchen that goes *rangbab kyi samten chenpo*, which can be translated as "the great meditation of the natural state." This is considered the most supreme meditation, and yet, it is simply resting in the uncontrived, unaltered state of mind as it is, which is already free and enlightened.

Sometimes the idea that the nature of the mind is already enlightened might be hard for people to comprehend. For ordinary people, if there were a hypothetical argument between one voice asserting that the nature of the mind is enlightened and another denying it, the latter would likely be more convincing. When most people think of their mind, they don't think that its nature is enlightened. All they see is the unenlightened, complex state of their mind, filled with fear, worry, judgment, and so forth. Some people might respond, "What are you talking about? Nature of mind enlightened? No way! Not my mind."

Yet, when people go on a meditation retreat and practice simply sitting in silence and not doing anything with the mind—not trying to purify the mind, cultivate virtues, have wholesome thoughts, or engage with experiences—the mind becomes free, spacious, and peaceful on its own. Even profound insight arises by itself in the mind. This is why people go on meditation retreats in the first place. This is the most convincing evidence that the nature of the mind is enlightened. Otherwise, if we are just sitting and doing nothing, the mind could descend into more negativity. But this is not the case.

Dzogchen meditation is, in the end, the art of nondoing rather than doing, or exerting effort to arrive at an imagined destination somewhere in the realm of our consciousness.

What we are seeking is always closer than we think. Sometimes we don't see it because it seems so ordinary, too subtle, or too close. Freedom is always within our reach when we look for it in the right place.

The Value of Meditation Guidance

Once, during one of my trips to South Korea, a friend of mine, a Korean Buddhist monk and fluent English speaker, told me a story. A company invited a well-respected Zen master to give a talk and lead a meditation session for its employees. Many people in that audience were very new to meditation. The teacher simply gave the usual Zen meditation instruction: "Just sit." He didn't say much more than that, so people became very lost and didn't know what to do. They started fidgeting around and so forth.

In the West, often at meditation retreats, the teachers tend to offer clear, step-by-step guidance on meditation. This is a great model to adopt, even in a book. For beginners, listening to a guided meditation instruction from a meditation teacher is extremely helpful. Especially in Dzogchen, receiving meditation guidance from a living meditation teacher is essential. Rigpa, or nondual awareness, is not conceptual. It is not something our thinking mind can easily grasp. Therefore, through guidance from a living teacher, we may be able to open our mind and drop into a zone inside us in which we can completely understand and experience rigpa.

Also, human communication is not 100 percent verbal. There is also nonverbal communication that comes through someone, such as their energy field, facial expression, tone of voice, and so on. A Dzogchen meditation teacher may be able to tune in to us and offer what we need to hear, which is something perhaps books or apps cannot do. Even if one is already a well-seasoned meditator, it can be very beneficial to hear live meditation guidance from someone now and then.

There is a lineage called *dzogchen nyengyü*, which can literally be translated as "the hearing lineage" or "oral lineage." Sometimes in this tradition, the Dzogchen master does not use any text when offering ngotröd or meditation guidance. Instead, they speak spontaneously to communicate with the meditator sitting there. What is transmitted is more than the words—their tone of voice, body language, and presence all become a powerful medium for communication.

Meditation Guidance

In the appendix at the back of the book, you will find a link to audio meditation instructions as well as written instructions. A recommended practice session might include:

- prayers, such as the refuge prayer;
- setting an intention;
- meditation session;
- compassion practice, such as loving-kindness; and
- dedication of the merits.

Navigating the Inner Journey

གང་ལ་གོལ་བསྒྲུ་མ་གོལ་ལམ་གྱི་གནད། །
ཕྱི་རུ་འཕྲོ་ཞིང་འཕྱོར་རྐྱེན་དང་སྦྱོར་མེལ། །
ནང་དུ་རྨོངས་འཐིབས་རྨུགས་འགྱོད་ཐེ་ཚོམ་ལ། །
ཕེས་པ་ཁ་ཡན་ཐཿ གྱི་གསེང་ལ་བསྒོམ། །
མཆམ་བཞག་ལྟ་སྟངས་འཛིན་འཆིང་ཤིགས་ལ་ཞོག །
མི་ཡེངས་མི་བསྒོམ་གློད་དེ་ཤིག་གེར་ཞོག །

Not falling into any pitfalls and deceptions is a key point of the path.
When the mind goes outward and is scattered and restless, clear it by maintaining the natural state.
When the mind is lost inwardly in dullness, obscuration, regret, and doubt,
clear it by PHAD, and then meditate in that state.
Let go of grasping and fixation by resting in the manner of meditative equipoise.
Without distraction and without meditating, relax in the state of ease.

9

The Dance of the Inner Maras

Things are not always supposed to go smoothly in this part of the galaxy. Every endeavor has its own twists and turns. It's as if this is built into the law of nature, like Murphy's Law: what can go wrong will go wrong. This idea may sound very pessimistic when simply hearing it without looking at the bigger picture. However, the small and large struggles that occur in our endeavors are sometimes the very things that make our lives richer, especially when we are not completely defeated by them. Without a doubt, this life is literally a hero's or heroine's journey. We must learn how to love such a journey along with its struggles.

Even our spiritual journey is not always like walking on a flower-strewn path. It has its own struggles and often comes with unexpected obstacles. These obstacles are not totally meaningless episodes, like a cosmic spell that we wish had never occurred in the first place. They can sometimes defeat us, and then we descend into the lowest dimension of our consciousness. On the other hand, if we look into them and keep them in check, then ironically, they can be a source of spiritual awakening—inner understanding, purification, and the development of wisdom. They can even be a doorway to transcendence.

Meeting with Mara

When obstacles visit us, we should not always think they are a personal phenomenon. They are part of the spiritual journey shared by many people. Even the masters of the past, whom we hold in the highest regard, could not avoid encountering them. In the Buddhist sutras, there is a character called Mara, depicted in various forms according to people's wild imaginations. In some ways, Mara can be considered the equivalent of the devil.

Yet Mara is not regarded as a being outside ourselves but rather as an allegorical representation of the human ego and everything that binds us to the prison of suffering, holding us back from awakening. The ancient Buddhist texts warn us that as spiritual beings, we must expect that Mara is already planning to play pranks on us.

The idea of Mara can be applied to all the obstacles that arise in our meditation practice. But keep in mind that Mara is not some demonic being who is separate from our own mind. The brilliant twelfth-century Tibetan master Machig Labdron made sure that Mara should not be understood as a spooky, supernatural being but rather as an archetypal representation of our ego and attachment. In her writings, she stated that Mara is not an enormous, scary, demonic creature. Instead, she said, "The so-called Mara is whatever is creating obstacles to liberation."

The very heart of Buddhist tantra is nonduality, transcending any intrinsic duality between good and bad, the divine and the devil, Buddha and Mara. Machig Labdron also stated, "Realize Mara is dharmakaya! Then you conquer the concept of Mara." What she said perfectly illuminates the nonduality between Mara and dharmakaya, the ultimate Buddha.

This stands in contrast to theistic traditions that have no common ground between the devil and the divine. In some traditions, the devil is intrinsically bad and will never be good. But that is not true in Tantric Buddhism. There are some fantastic stories in ancient Buddhist scriptures about a powerful Mara named Rudra, who was originally a monk. He lost his way and strayed from the path, becoming a very egotistical, powerful being among all the humans and gods. Finally, he was tamed by *heruka*s, the "wrathful buddhas," and eventually became a *dharmapala*, a "benevolent protector." It was even prophesied that one day he would become an enlightened Buddha.

This story affirms that Mara is not intrinsically evil; it also has divinity. Therefore, all the obstacles that arise on the journey, such as doubt, fear, and so forth, are not intrinsically bad. Their true nature is as pure as love and wisdom. If we are able to embrace them with wisdom and nondual awareness, they will not bind us. Instead, they can become the fuel that expedites the process of awakening.

But sometimes, it is humorous as well as illuminating to personify obstacles in the image of Mara. If we describe meditative obstacles in that way, Mara is both challenging and cunningly deceptive. Mara is challenging when it manifests in uncomfortable situations like fear, confusion, and doubt that arise in our meditation practice. At other times, it is deceptive when beautiful meditation experiences arise, like the nyam we described earlier. Mara wants to trap you in either challenging, painful situations or seductively pleasant experiences.

Once, Patrul Rinpoche was on his way to do a meditation retreat, and he went to see his guru, Jigme Gyalwé Nyugu, who said, "It seems this time you are going to encounter serious challenges. You will have to be very vigilant, or you will not be able to go beyond them." Patrul Rinpoche went on to do his retreat. One day, suddenly, it began to rain heavily, along with earth-shaking thunder and lightning, which totally terrified him. He thought he might be killed by it. Finally, the skies cleared, and he saw a rainbow shining. Then, a nomad woman appeared with a container of milk as an offering. Patrul Rinpoche thought maybe it was an auspicious omen, and he was very happy.

The next day, Patrul Rinpoche went to see his master, who asked, "Did you run into any serious challenges?"

Patrul Rinpoche said, "No, I didn't encounter any of them."

His master said to him, "Tell me the details of your retreat."

Patrul Rinpoche described what happened. The teacher responded, "When you were scared that you would be killed, that was the Mara of self-deceit. When you were happy that someone offered you milk, that was the Mara of elation." Basically, his guru said that he failed to go beyond the challenges.

Patrul Rinpoche had some idea that challenges were much more powerful, like huge internal confusion. He never thought that these reactions to small events were a form of Mara. The fact that even Patrul Rinpoche, who was an extraordinary spiritual being, fell prey to Mara is a humbling reminder that we too can be trapped by Mara more easily than we might expect.

In some sense, not just individuals but an entire spiritual community can be trapped by Mara, which reminds me of this funny story. One time, Mara decided to go on vacation after corrupting the minds of many people. He and his attendant were strolling along with ease in the countryside of India. His attendant noticed that a meditator had just become enlightened by seeing the truth. Mara didn't react, and then his attendant was perplexed, since his master usually became extremely upset when he saw that someone had realized the truth. His attendant couldn't resist doing something. He jumped in front of Mara and said, "My Lord, did you see that the meditator just realized the truth?"

Mara replied, "Well, yes, I saw it. But first of all, we are on vacation. And second, don't worry. Soon people will make a dogma out of it."

The Inner Mara of Ego

The spiritual path can be seen as a hero's journey on which we should not be too relaxed or overly complacent, thinking that it is the smoothest, most beautiful, and challenge-free voyage. It is definitely *not* like going to France on vacation. Some level of struggle is to be expected; otherwise, we would not call it the hero's or heroine's journey.

The spiritual path and meditation practice itself are where we will meet our inner Maras. So Mara is, in some way, part of the spiritual journey. It can be regarded as our traveling companion who now and then irritates us, causes us headaches, and also tries to smooth-talk us out of the journey.

This cunning and stubborn nature of the ego is acknowledged by some of the most enlightened masters. For example, Dzogchen master Shabkar wrote a song in which he personified ego and innate wisdom. They had a chat, and innate wisdom began to chastise ego. Wisdom perceived ego as an affront and combative, and ego argued back that he would win eventually in a war with wisdom. Ego argued that even though spiritual people, monks, and nuns all give lip service to wisdom, as if they were devoted to wisdom, they were his (ego's) subjects, and he had control over them. The song is filled with a lot of humor. In the same way, now and then, we can find humor in discovering our own internal conflict between light and darkness, as long as we don't identify with our ego.

However, the everyday consciousness of many people is mainly driven by ego and a host of the usual repetitive thoughts and emotions. This may sound like I am portraying humanity's consciousness quite poorly. Of course, we also experience beautiful and even sublime states of mind all the time. Some of these are spiritual, while others are simply positive states, such as joy, appreciation, love, and kindness.

But when it comes to anything related to the ego, it's not so easy to recognize what is happening in us. The ego dominates our lives, and we are unconscious of its power over us unless we are willing to do some deep inner work. As we bring awareness into our daily lives to the best of our ability, we not only begin to see the games of the ego, but its grip also starts to loosen. This is a time when you can call yourself a Dzogchen yogi, if you want to, because you deserve it. Until then, you might want to have reservations about giving yourself such a title.

Five Hindrances

There are five hindrances, or obscurations, that can occur in our meditation practice. These five hindrances are like manifestations of Mara that can block us from experiencing stillness, insight, and inner awakening. There are various ways to categorize and order the five hindrances. Many traditional Tibetan Buddhist texts categorize them in this order: sensory desire, ill will, sloth and torpor, restlessness and regret, and doubt.

Generally speaking, whenever we encounter these, we can remember that we are dealing with Mara. Or if they become really powerful, we can think of them as the army of Mara. There are also different ways to personify them other than the powerful archetype of Mara.

Nagarjuna addressed them as thieves or robbers who steal one's true meditation experience as well as the opportunity to actualize inner liberation. Nagarjuna said,

> Restlessness and regret, ill will, sloth and torpor,
> sensory desire, and doubt—
> understand that these five obscurations
> are thieves who plunder the wealth of virtue!

These five hindrances are mental states that arise in our meditation practice as well as in our daily life. When they arise in ordinary life, we are often not conscious of them and may let them run the show, dominating our mind completely. In meditation, we become more aware of their presence, which gives us the chance to choose not to give in to them. These five states are very human mental states that people go through in their lives. Numerous human experiences can bind us, but these five are the most common. They are not esoteric neuroses; we are quite familiar with them. Some Buddhist texts describe them as the kleshas or neuroses of beings in the human world, which is often called the realm of desire.

In general, we are experiencing thoughts, emotions, and moods all the time, which is the characteristic of being alive. Many of our experiences are not always positive or even virtuous. The mind produces thousands of thoughts each day, many of which are negative and repetitive due to a principle known as the "negativity bias." This is not a shocking discovery in human psychology. Even in daily life, we are often caught up in worry, agitation, and judgment as normal, as if there is nothing wrong with that.

So these five states are very common states of mind that you or your neighbor experience. These categories are psychologically brilliant, showing that early Buddhists really understood the state of the human mind.

Sensory Desire

The first hindrance is sensory desire. It is our desire to experience the pleasures of the senses. There is nothing intrinsically wrong with such desire, so this should not lead us to hold some life-denying philosophy asserting that desire is fundamentally bad or the corrupter of the human soul. It is part of our existence that literally blesses life and the world with the beauty we want to taste.

This hindrance is more about indulging in and becoming completely caught up in our desires. This can not only create obstacles to spiritual awakening but can also cause tremendous suffering even at a psychological level. Imagine that you are practicing meditation on a retreat, either alone or with a group of people. You might start craving delicious food or complain that they are not serving food that satisfies your senses. Or maybe you are so attached to the delicious food at the retreat that your focus becomes more on the food than on meditation. You may be imagining sensual pleasures and craving them, or you may actually be indulging in them in the moment. Both modes can be hindrances to your practice.

In everyday life, we often indulge in pleasure through our five senses so much that we are not only addicted to them but also use them as a pacifier to avoid unconscious feelings. We cover up feelings like boredom and insecurity by indulging in sense pleasures. This, again, does not mean we should always suppress sense desires when they arise or prevent ourselves from enjoying the delights of ordinary life. It is about being mindful of their arising and consciously making sure we are not ruled by them.

Those who have done a semi-fasting retreat (eating only in the morning) often realize how much they have been indulging in all kinds of sensual pleasures to fill the emptiness in their hearts, becoming enslaved by them. At first, they go through a struggle with the desire for pleasure; then sooner or later, they experience an amazing liberation where they are no longer bound by their desires. Instead, they find an incredible sense of joy and peace that lies beneath the empty heart. That is our true heart.

For example, when I was a monk, I practiced semi-fasting while attending a monsoon retreat in the Vinaya system, which lasts for many weeks. One of the guiding precepts of the retreat is not to eat from the afternoon until sunrise the next day. As a teenage monk, this was very difficult for me at first. I felt really hungry and tormented inside. I even had a bit of anger toward the retreat, which was a conflict for me. The retreat was supposed to be holy, but I was also angry about it. It was almost an experience of cognitive dissonance. After a while, it became natural to fast that way. I felt a strong sense of well-being, both physically and mentally. When the retreat was ready to end, I felt some grief, not wanting to leave the retreat. This experience gave me insight into how much we are attached to sensory pleasures and may be missing the deeper sense of joy of life that comes from reconnecting with the essence of who we are.

Some Buddhist temples chant liturgies to bless the meal. Some of the verses remind us that we are eating food so that we can practice the Dharma, the Buddhist path. This can strike us as asceticism, denying pleasure that might come from food. However, it should be understood differently. Perhaps the true message of the verses is not that pleasure from food is meaningless or that we shouldn't enjoy it. It is more about not allowing our consciousness to descend by indulging in the senses. These liturgies are mainly influenced by the Vinaya, the Buddhist monastic system, which emphasizes a life of simplicity and the virtue of monasticism.

The attitude of Vajrayana, or Tantric Buddhism, is completely different. It teaches us to regard our body as a mandala or a holy temple, ourselves as a deity, and food as an offering. It invites us to see the sacredness in sensual pleasures. Ultimately, the Tantric Buddhist attitude toward the sensory delights is healthy and goes along with the very rhythm of life itself. It is not built on some religious morality invented by certain people at a certain time.

Many of us like to go to places like Italy and France, especially cities like Paris, which have beautiful buildings, castles, and museums that please our eyes and mesmerize our minds. We should be very happy that Paris exists for humanity because it is a place to experience the delights of life and enjoy sensory pleasures.

It would be terrible if there were a religious code that said you should not visit Paris.

Enjoying pleasure doesn't have to be extravagant or tastelessly ostentatious. It can be as simple as walking along the Seine River and having a cup of coffee at a café, looking at the beautiful buildings. Or walking on the beach somewhere on an island in Hawai'i with bare feet, watching the evening sunset. In the end, life is not always about being lost in grand ideas about what we should be doing. We can enjoy each moment with its simple pleasures, like listening to music or drinking tea, which are naturally pleasing to our senses. The act of enjoying the senses can be sacred when viewed as a ritual of celebrating our existence and life itself.

This hindrance isn't so much about enjoying sense pleasures as it is about being completely trapped by the desire for them, making them an obstacle to spiritual development. You could be an ascetic in the mountains yet still be lost in endless desire and fantasies, which can then bring your consciousness down and prevent you from experiencing inner transformation.

Ill Will

The next hindrance is ill will, which is our thought or intention to harm others or even wishing that harmful or unfavorable circumstances would occur in the lives of other people. For many spiritual people, ill will is such a negative category that they may have an unconscious resistance to recognizing it in themselves. There are others who indulge in ill will without having any sense of conscience about it at all.

Ill will is not only a factor of violence, abuse, or aggression directed toward others, but it also causes a tremendous amount of internal pain in the one holding the ill will. First, we need to recognize it in ourselves and see if we harbor it. Then we may want to apply a method of inquiry to look into its cause. Finally, we will be ready to work on letting it go.

Often, ill will is caused by some external situation that happened in our lives in relation to others. Our lives are quite entangled with many people; they are relational, and not all our interactions and relationships with others will always go well, smoothly, or have a happy ending. Due to complex factors, we get along with some people, whether friends, relatives, coworkers, or romantic partners. Then we tend to have well-wishes toward them and even the intention to help them. Such relationships are not only a source of happiness but are also necessary for our survival. Harmonious relationships with others are, in many ways, the foundation of universal morality. This is also why people feel altruism, selflessness, generosity, caring, trust, and so forth.

On the other hand, we sometimes have conflicts with others, not due to one singular factor but from many complex factors. It's always a mystery why we get along with some people and not others. Perhaps you have experienced trying to be nice to someone to win their heart, yet no matter how hard you tried, that person kept turning you into their enemy. There seemed to be zero potential in their consciousness to open their heart and see your goodness. When that happens, it can be so disappointing that we may feel ashamed, inadequate, or develop ill will toward that person.

A lot of ill will comes from unfortunate situations between ourselves and others, where someone has hurt us in varying degrees. Our feeling of ill will becomes moral and reasonable—even a form of righteousness. Without looking more deeply, ill will and hatred toward someone can seem logical, as if this might eventually accomplish something useful. But the truth is that ill will doesn't accomplish anything constructive. Instead, it eats at us inside in a way that can torment us.

Ill will is a major stumbling block in personal and spiritual evolution. As long as our consciousness is filled with ill will, it would be very difficult to grow our hearts into love and compassion in an authentic way. Unfortunately, sometimes people act out their ill will toward others, which can lead to very regrettable actions.

In meditation practice, whenever someone pops up in our head whom we have ill will or resentment toward, our mind is usually thrown off-balance. Then, instead of resting in peace or stillness, our mind is fighting a war with people who may not even be physically nearby. We are declaring war against these invisible beings in our heads.

Working with Ill Will

When ill will arises in meditation, there are different methodologies for working with it. You can use antidotes to ill will, such as developing compassion and understanding toward that person. In a more direct way, you can simply witness it without identifying with it. As long as you do not identify with it, the hindrance will lose its power to grip you.

On one of my trips to Korea, I visited Jeju Island, which is beautiful and filled with history. When I landed there, I was amazed by the beauty of nature and loved the towns. Then my friends took me to visit a cave where a group of people had starved to death. They informed me that thousands of people were killed on that island by the government, but a group had escaped to the cave and eventually died from starvation. It is such a tragic story. I could not believe that human beings could be so hateful and heartless toward each other.

We performed a ceremony of offering food to the dead, and I chanted the Dzogchen liturgy called "Buddha Samantabhadra's Prayer" by Rigdzin Gödem. While chanting it, I came across the verse that explains the genesis of hatred. It explains that hatred arises from the illusion of separation and not recognizing the true nature of reality. It reminds us that violence and war do not ultimately come from political and social issues but from the unawakened state of our consciousness. And peace will come not from modifying external circumstances but from the spiritual awakening of consciousness.

The Root Cause of Ill Will

In the end, it is important to look into the root of ill will. It all comes down to our ego, which wants to hold on to suffering and does everything in its power to resist love and liberation. Without ego, it is impossible to harbor hatred. Ego is the sense of a separate self who feels that "someone has done something to *me*" or "*I* don't like them, so *I* can hate them." As long as we are trapped by our ego, it will always find someone or something to hate.

Sometimes, if someone presents even the slightest challenge to the ego, it can react strongly, feeling insulted, ridiculed, and attacked, and indulging in ever-scorching hatred inside. It is very easy to lose our intelligence, common sense, or heart when the ego feels challenged by even small matters that might take place in a conversation with someone.

Once, there was a yogi who achieved what are called *siddhi*s, the ability to perform miracles. One of them was the ability to multiply himself any number of times. He realized that soon his time on earth would be up, and Yamaraja, the Lord of Death, would be coming to get him. Soon, his prediction came true, and he heard a knock on the door. He knew it was the Lord of Death, so he immediately multiplied himself into 108 identical copies. He thought he could trick the Lord of Death, who wouldn't know which was the real one to take away.

The Lord of Death entered the house and was perplexed at first. He couldn't find the person he was looking for because all the people looked the same. But the Lord of Death knew the weakness of the human ego and came up with a smart idea. He said, "It's amazing that you are such a great magician that you can multiply yourself. You all look the same. But there's one thing wrong..."

As soon as the yogi heard that, he couldn't control himself, got angry, and jumped out of the crowd, shouting, "What's wrong?!"

Yamaraja grabbed him by the neck and took him away from this world.

The ego is not only the source of ill will toward others, but it also causes us to suffer. Without any concrete reason, the ego can harbor an aversion or a sense of repulsion toward a person or a group of people, without even knowing any of them personally. This can then turn into ill will or hatred. Because the ego finds them repulsive through some twisted logic, one naturally feels there is every reason to hate them. This kind of ill will is more than an individual issue; it is the basis of collective hatred, such as xenophobia and prejudice.

Sloth and Torpor

Sloth and torpor are very similar and represent a lack of enthusiasm and joy, accompanied by drowsiness and lethargy. As we practice meditation, there are moments when our mind doesn't want to engage with the practice and just wants to check out. Various factors might cause us to feel sleepy and lack enthusiasm while meditating. The cause might be physical, but it can also be psychological.

For example, if someone is not an experienced meditator, sitting and doing nothing might be so boring to the mind that it just wants to take a nap. In general, meditation is very inspiring when you know how to practice it. However, it can also be unfamiliar to the mind, which tends to be busy, active, and engaged with thoughts. When people love to do something, they tend to have a lot of energy from that enthusiasm. Just think about how much time people spend on social media or video games with their minds very alert and engaged. Therefore, much of the sleepiness and lethargy that arise during meditation practice often come from psychological rather than purely biological causes.

Another reason this hindrance arises is that even if we know how to meditate, our mind has some unconscious resistance to being fully present in the moment and doesn't know how to break its addiction to thinking. We tend to try to escape from the present if our mind is not interested in what we are experiencing at that moment.

Sloth and torpor become obstacles in meditation practice if they are not dealt with. Let's say you are in a meditation retreat and dozing off all the time. If you neglect to look into it, that drowsiness, sleepiness, and dullness will keep you from experiencing stillness, insight, and awareness.

Specific techniques to help with drowsiness during meditation include opening your eyes wide and gazing into the light. If that doesn't help, you might want to try getting up, walking around, or doing some stretches until you feel alert enough to return and continue meditating.

This hindrance can also be interpreted as a state of mind that impacts our everyday life, such as a lack of enthusiasm and inspiration for embracing each moment. It comes with a sense of the drudgery of daily life. Overcoming it allows us to find a sense of joy in each day and even love what we are doing.

One method to bring more liveliness to each moment is to be grateful for the simplest things—appreciating that we are breathing, that we are alive, and that we are paying attention to the ordinariness of each moment. Something as simple as walking your dog outside allows you to feel that you are living your life; no grand achievement is required to feel satisfied.

Restlessness

Restlessness is a state of having so many thoughts and so much emotional turmoil that it prevents us from sitting still in awareness while meditating. Our mind can sometimes be overactive and totally lost in mental proliferation—anticipating the future, remembering events that occurred long ago that have no relevance to the present, or talking to people in our mind, some of whom might already be dead, and picturing all kinds of scenarios that either make us jubilant or uncomfortable. When we are distracted and lost in our thinking mind, we are completely disconnected from the present moment. This is also a hindrance in everyday life, not just during meditation.

Releasing the Knot of the Mind

Sometimes there are stories about people who go on a meditation retreat and get lost in this state of restlessness. They make all kinds of plans in their mind, such as redesigning their kitchen counter, including visualizing the materials to buy, which store to go to, which contractors to hire, the budget, and so forth. Then they visualize themselves as a happy person standing next to their new smooth granite or marble kitchen counter. Before you know it, the meditation session has ended, and this fantasy was all that they achieved.

If we lose awareness, the mind can go anywhere. There is no limit to the fantasies that the mind can create. A mindfulness teacher from the Theravada tradition once told me that in their community, they coined the term "vipassana romance." This came from real situations when people were practicing vipassana in a meditation retreat. One person would catch sight of someone and find that they were attracted to that person. Without even exchanging one word, that person would fall in love and imagine dating, getting married, and having a life with the object of their fantasy. There is obvious humor in this. It's a paradox since we assume that people would not get so lost in a mundane fantasy while on a meditation retreat.

The truth is that no matter where we are or what we are doing, we are just human beings with this wild mind. Without awareness, our mind can be as unruly as ever, and we can easily get trapped in its creations, even during meditation. As long as we are lost in our whirling sea of thoughts, even though we might be in a very good meditative posture, we are not really meditating at all.

Restlessness as a Distracted Mind

A Buddhist parable depicts the power of being mindful and being distracted. Once, an athlete and a performing artist were going to have a wrestling match. The performer was extremely intimidated by this powerful athlete, who wore a precious gem on his forehead as an ornament. The performer went back home and cried to his wife, saying, "If I wrestle with that athlete tomorrow, he will certainly kill me."

His wife said, "Don't worry. I have a strategy."

The next day, the performer went to wrestle with the athlete, and his wife followed him. The two men began to wrestle. Suddenly, the performer's wife began to shout and sing these words:

> Even though you, athlete, are powerful,
> the gem on your forehead is ready to fall off.

At that moment, the athlete got distracted, and the performing artist took that opportunity to defeat him. Then the athlete made a statement:

> I, the athlete who lost mindfulness and vigilance, was defeated
> by a weaker man who had concentration.
> I haven't seen a more cunning and deceptive enemy than
> this distracted mind.

Regret

Regret is linked with restlessness as one hindrance because regret is a form of restlessness. Regret can be quite unsettling when we are stuck in it. It is often used by the ego to perpetuate emotional pain, even though there is no merit in doing so. This is not to say that we should remove regret completely from our system. There is a healthy regret that can be a form of conscience, which can bring emotional release and healing. But often, regret is just the ego's resistance to inner liberation, and we will continue to have regret until we realize that.

Remember that this is not an invitation to bypass regret. There is a spiritual way of experiencing regret that can be a powerful part of letting go. An example is the Vajrasattva meditation. This is a Tibetan Buddhist tantric practice for the purification of all our negative habits and the effects of negative deeds.

In this practice, we allow ourselves to feel regret for everything that we have done wrong, not just externally but internally as well, such as indulging in delusions, judgments, and anger. Then at some point, we visualize that pure nectar comes from Vajrasattva's body, enters our body, and washes away all the negativities from our body and mind. They become pristine and cleansed. Then we imagine that Vajrasattva smiles upon us and utters a verse of assurance, saying that now we are purified.

This is an example of how sometimes regret can be useful for inner healing and letting go. There is a point in that practice where we also let go of regret and allow ourselves to feel that our whole consciousness is no longer veiled by the impact of our past negativities.

This hindrance, like the others, is also relevant to our daily life. If we are able to work with it in our meditation practice, we may be able to become free of it for the rest of our lives. Otherwise, regret can be an emotional and spiritual hindrance, whether we are meditating or not. It can bite us from the inside and cause silent emotional pain, hindering us from appreciating our present life and moving forward.

Often, regret can become a lifeless compulsion when it becomes an emotional fixation. Imagine someone living their whole life with regret about not making the right choice when they were younger or thinking they should have chosen a different path. But the truth is that there is nothing we can do about past events. We cannot go back into the past in a time machine and redo it, except in science fiction. In this example, regret is not only useless and keeps us contracted, it also does not produce any concrete, positive outcome. Sometimes our regret is like a block that closes our heart. When we let go of it, a river of joy erupts from our heart, and we feel more alive than ever.

We might like to hold the aspiration that we can live a life that is not bound by unhealthy regret. Imagine that someday we will die, not tormented by regret but feeling that our heart is completely fulfilled. As long as we are haunted by regret, we will not enjoy this unbelievably beautiful yet transitory life on earth. Regret is an inner chain that can and should be broken.

Doubt

Doubt is a natural process of our mind trying to figure out a situation or determine whether we can believe or trust something or someone. Now and then, doubt can have an aspect of intelligence.

As a hindrance, doubt refers to any lack of conviction that creates obstacles on one's spiritual path. Doubt can be such a huge impediment that it may even cause one to stop the entire journey.

It can be a powerful form of Mara if we don't cut through it and go beyond it.

For example, one could have a big doubt about one's capacity for spiritual awakening. Such doubt can be very convincing when it is unchecked. It is like the devil's advocate who has some of the best logical evidence that you should quit the spiritual journey once and forever. Sometimes doubt masquerades as wisdom, even though it is purely the ego's game, using ignorance of our true nature in order to stop the journey.

To overcome this hindrance, we can apply the Buddhist doctrine of *tathagatagarbha*, or "buddha nature," which says that the true nature of each of us is already a buddha. Because of this nature, we all have the inborn capacity to become fully awakened.

Doubt can take many forms. As long as it hinders us from becoming awakened, it is a form of Mara, one of the five hindrances. It is important for us to recognize it right away if it arises during our meditation practice. Some Buddhist teachers are adamant that it is not sufficient to memorize the list of hindrances; rather, we need to recognize them whenever they arise in our mind.

Imagine that you are on a meditation retreat, and you allow yourself to doubt whether meditation practice is meaningful. You might start to think that perhaps you are wasting your time doing spiritual hocus-pocus instead of making money or enjoying a vacation in some idyllic place. If you allow this doubt to take over your mind, it may hinder you from finding serenity and insight.

Such doubt tends to go away once we truly taste the power of meditation practice. One time, I was co-leading a mindfulness meditation retreat. I was assigned to meet with a small group of people to listen to their experiences and answer their questions. There was a man in the group who appeared to be an average Joe, someone who I would not have thought was a meditator if I had simply seen him on the street. He shared that he got into mindfulness meditation because he had previously been suffering a lot. Meditation changed his life, and he wished he had known about it a long time ago. He said this with such trust and faith in his meditation practice, which was very inspiring for me to witness. There was zero doubt in him when he spoke. He was not speaking from his head but from his direct personal experience, which was filled with so much conviction.

10

Overcoming Hindrances

There are many methods in the Buddhist tradition for overcoming the five hindrances, but some of them are not really life-affirming and may not be suitable for everyone.

The Dzogchen method of dealing with hindrances differs significantly from the orthodox Buddhist teachings. For example, when a desire arises, it can be another transitory feeling that goes away, or it can be a powerful one that throws us off-balance. Instead of applying complex, life-negating methods, we can welcome the desire with the sacred attitude that it is a display of rigpa, or *rigpé rol tsal*. We continuously ground ourselves in open awareness and do not tinker with the desire, neither following it nor getting rid of it. Then desire becomes just another pure experience that is neither good nor bad.

As we practice in this way, we develop a harmonious relationship with desires and all of the other hindrances. They no longer have the power to bind us because we stop giving our power to them. We are able to overcome hindrances simply by applying this utterly simple method, which is nothing more than pure witnessing.

The definition of the first hindrance is not just desire itself but includes allowing oneself to be completely ruled by desire, which is a form of attachment. When that attachment leaves our system, desire becomes a pure experience like any other natural experience since there is nothing intrinsically wrong with it.

The same logic applies to the other hindrances as well. From the Dzogchen point of view, whenever we are not lost in experiences, whether positive or negative, that state of consciousness is considered liberation, the dharmakaya, the mind of the Primordial Buddha.

One could say that Dzogchen has a very affirming, nondual, and holistic way of dealing with the hindrances. It doesn't view them as evil antagonists; instead, it embraces them as pure human experiences and holds a sacred outlook that regards them as the miraculous display of rigpa.

Thus, the method becomes utterly simple—simply witnessing the hindrances the moment they arise, whether desire, doubt, or something else. Then we do not judge them as bad but see them as another movement in our consciousness. In that recognition, our unconscious habit to indulge and identify with the impulse, such as desire and so forth, will dissolve naturally on its own.

Arising and Liberating

This method of witnessing is called simultaneous arising and liberation, *shardrol dünyam*, an important method in Dzogchen. There is nothing conceptual about it. It is totally experiential. You can use this method and taste the immediate impact right there on the spot. It is considered the Dzogchen way of remaining in awareness and not getting lost in endless human experiences, which can be colorful, sometimes messy and trivial, and every now and then, ecstatic or even spiritual.

If we break down the phrase into terms, *arising* refers to an immediate occurrence of thoughts, emotions, or external stimuli. The term *liberation* is a state of mind where you are not bound by anything that arises but instead experience whatever arises in a more awakened state of mind, or pure awareness. Usually, thoughts and emotions are popping up in us all the time on their own, and they are also often triggered by our engagement with external stimuli, such as sound, sight, movement, or a particular situation.

There is a story about Padmasambhava who went to study with the Dzogchen master Shri Singha. In their initial meeting, Shri Singha pointed his finger upward toward the sky and uttered this instruction twice:

Whatever arises, do not grasp at it.
Whatever arises, do not grasp at it.

This was Shri Singha's way of showing the quintessence of the entire Dzogchen teachings. Not only is this utterance profound and pithy, but pointing his finger into the sky has symbolic significance. The sky represents the big mind, or rigpa, or dharmadhatu, the dimension of reality as it is, unconditioned by our thinking mind. Shri Singha is saying that the way to liberation is to drop into rigpa and welcome everything that arises in the moment. There is nothing more to do beyond that. You experience that your mind is completely free while experiencing life that spins on its own.

Releasing the Knot of the Mind

Disrupting the Force of Hindrances

In this doha, Dudjom Lingpa gives a simple yet powerful technique for overcoming the five hindrances from the Dzogchen point of view. He says that if our mind gets lost in outer sensory stimuli, thoughts, or emotions, or becomes extremely busy and restless, the method is simply to recognize this mental activity without trying to get rid of it and just drop into awareness itself.

The hindrances may then continue for a while, but they will lack the power to influence our mind. They become another display of rigpa itself. Sooner or later, they will dissolve without any trace, much like a bird that leaves no trace of tracks in the sky.

Power of PHAD!

If you feel too inward, becoming sleepy, dull, or lethargic, lacking clarity and energy, then Dudjom Lingpa recommends exclaiming the PHAD syllable to alert your mind. Shouting "PHAD" can help reenergize your mind and bring it back to the present moment.

As we described in an earlier chapter, the syllable PHAD is widely used in many Tibetan Buddhist practices, such as Chöd. Machig Labdron said that PHAD has different meanings; there's not one absolute definition of it. While there is a philosophical meaning to the syllable PHAD, we don't need to get caught up in it. Instead, we simply use this method to stop being lost in thoughts and, particularly, to bring alertness to our mind or to stop the thinking mind immediately. The meditator can also use this technique to drop into rigpa right away by shattering the thinking mind. Some Dzogchen masters may use the PHAD syllable even when they are pointing out rigpa to the meditator.

Overcoming Hindrances

There is also a particular way of exclaiming the PHAD syllable in the Dzogchen tradition. As Patrul Rinpoche wrote,

Suddenly let out a mind-shattering "PHAD!"
Fierce, forceful, and abrupt. Amazing!

This is how we are supposed to exclaim "PHAD." When we exclaim "PHAD" in such a way, it creates an energetic shockwave through our system that literally disrupts the continuous state of the thinking mind. In that moment, the mind becomes alert, fully present, and there are not so many thoughts. This simple technique can help us avoid falling prey to the meditation hindrances, especially sleepiness and dullness. It can help us wake up energetically.

Short Periods, Many Times

There is a method, taught by some Dzogchen masters of the past, known in Tibetan as *yün tung drang mang*, or "short periods, many times." It is recommended for beginning meditators. In general, people who are new to meditation may run into many challenges, such as the five hindrances and others—being bored, uninterested, daydreaming, or lost in a mindless state. Just sitting in silence and doing nothing can initially be very difficult for many people. For some, this is the most tormenting thing to do, because there is no way to distract themselves. Even though someone may feel comfortable sitting in a meditation posture in silence, they may still be entertained by their thoughts or get stuck in a dull, zombie state of consciousness.

Therefore, if one keeps the meditation period short, then each time the session ends, there is a gap before the next session begins.

This gap allows us to restart the next session with much more freshness. It allows us to drop into awareness and stay in that state for a short while before some of the obstacles arise again to distract us.

For example, imagine that while you are meditating, you are sleeping a lot, dozing off all the time. In some ways, you are really not meditating, but you are not taking a siesta either. Instead of forcing yourself to continue to meditate, you can just take a little break, relax, and then restart the meditation practice again. You can hold these short periods of meditation many times a day. The period can be as short as a few minutes or longer, depending on what you need in order to avoid falling into the hindrances.

As time goes by, our mind develops the habit of meditating, and we can stay in awareness for longer periods without being challenged by the five hindrances.

The main point is to let your mind rest in its natural state, where you even let go of the idea that you are meditating or trying to manipulate the state of your mind. If you can simply abide in the natural state of mind, then hindrances can arise, but they will resolve by themselves. If they become more challenging, you can apply some of these simple methods to break free from them.

Resistance and Attachment

While we are meditating, it is very natural to have either resistance or attachment to our physical or emotional experiences and stimuli from outside. Sometimes, certain thoughts, physical sensations, or sights can be so delicious that we want to indulge in them. All we need to do is remind ourselves not to unconsciously or intentionally try to perpetuate them. There is no need to attempt to eradicate them either. We can enjoy the experiences until they dissolve by themselves.

On the other hand, resistance can happen in numerous ways, including not finding any pleasure or joy from silent sitting, which can lead to boredom. Or we might have unmet expectations of what we should be experiencing, and a little voice in the back of our head is disappointed.

When these resistances begin to influence your mind, recognize them, welcome them into your awareness, and soon they will be the same as the beautiful experiences. Then you won't feel pulled to get rid of them or escape from them.

Hindrances as Our GPS

In short, expect that these five hindrances will emerge in our meditation practice. This should not be interpreted as an indicator that we are doing something wrong or that our meditation practice is in bad shape. These categories can be helpful for recognizing them if they arise during meditation. That recognition can help us not succumb to them.

In some ways, the list of hindrances is like a meditation GPS. Some GPS technology is so smart that it constantly gives warnings about traffic, accidents, or radar ahead. Then the driver can take immediate action to avoid unpleasant situations. It's a useful tool. In the same way, these categories are a very useful tool to help meditators become aware of these hindrances when they arise.

Of course, part of us doesn't want to have them at all. Such a desire is a meditator's unreasonable fantasy that we should not entertain. Hindrances arise due to various factors, and they are not just happening during meditation. They are a manifestation of our consciousness that has a dimension we are aware of and a dimension we are not aware of. Some hindrances are already imprinted in our psyche, and they just keep surfacing, as long as the mental fuel for them doesn't run out.

Sometimes it can be wonderful to count the hindrances while we meditate because it gives us something to chew on. Just like any other endeavor, if there is no struggle, it can sometimes be boring. When we encounter the hindrances, we can recognize them right away, witness them, and not be caught by them. The moment we feel we have been liberated from them, there is a deep sense of wisdom, a little milestone of awakening.

Going Beyond Hindrances

These very human experiences that we come across in our meditation practice, which are labeled "hindrances," are not intrinsically bad or malevolent. It is important to remember that whenever we label experiences as hindrances, we are using that term as a way to recognize them when they occur. We should not turn that term into some type of validation of their evil nature. In the ultimate sense, there are no hindrances at all. The idea of "hindrance" is how we interpret situations, either internally or externally.

It is easy for our mind to turn these so-called hindrances into some eternal problem that we need to fight against. Even though we often treat the hindrances as obstacles on our spiritual path, they are not intrinsically obstacles, especially if we bring awareness to them. They can be a powerful fuel for inner growth.

In the Nyingma tradition, we perform a Vajrakilaya ceremony to remove so-called obstacles. Vajrakilaya is a wrathful tantric

Overcoming Hindrances

deity who holds a *phurba* (pronounced *purba*), or "dagger," that represents destroying all obstacles.

Once, I was having a conversation with a lama, and I told him, "I have lots of obstacles in my life."

He said, "Don't say that. If you say that, you will create the obstacles."

I thought that was amazing advice. It was very helpful for me to realize that often an "obstacle" is only my own interpretation of internal or external events in my life.

The next time I saw that lama, he gave me a very precious gift. It was a phurba, or dagger, made from a piece of an iron bridge built by the great fifteenth-century Mahasiddha Thangtong Gyalpo, known as Chakzampa, the Iron-Bridge Maker, who built fifty-four iron bridges in Tibet. Later, people in Tibet felt his bridges were blessed and often walked on them to find healing.

I placed that phurba on the altar at my home. It became a powerful reminder not to create too many narratives about obstacles. The true meaning of the Vajrakilaya practice and the significance of the phurba is to destroy all our fixation on the obstacles.

One of my lama friends loved collecting English expressions, and his students often taught him American English expressions. One of them was "chill out." He loved the phrase so much that he would suddenly say it in the middle of a talk or ceremony. Outwardly, he appeared to be joking as he said it with a big smile. But he was perhaps trying to remind people not to fixate on their problems or struggles.

So when you are looking into your hindrances and feel you need to fight against them or treat them as your adversaries, becoming really intense with them, just tell yourself, "Chill out!"

The Art of Living in Awareness

རྗེས་ཐོབ་དུས་ཀྱང་དེ་བཞིན་རང་སྐྱོང་ཞིང་། །
ལྟ་སྤྱོད་འགྲོ་འདུག་ལས་ཀ་གང་བྱེད་ཀྱང་། །
རང་ངོ་རིག་བཞིན་དྲན་ཤེས་སོ་མ་སྐྱོངས། །
ཡོད་མེད་བསམ་པའི་འཛིན་པ་གང་མེད་པས། །
མ་ཡེངས་ཡེངས་མེད་བསྒོམ་སྒོམ་འཛིན་འཛིན་མེད། །
དེའི་དང་མ་ཕོར་ཡོད་ལ་གང་བྱེད། །
གོལ་ནོར་ཕོར་ས་གང་ཡང་མེད་ཀྱང་བར། །
དགེ་སྦྱིག་བླང་དོར་མ་ནོར་གནད་གཅིག་གོ །

During post-meditation, one shall maintain the
natural state like that.
In whatever you do—view, conduct, and all
activities of going and staying—
maintain pristine mindfulness that is aware of
its own nature.

There is no clinging to thoughts of existence or nonexistence.
Continue undistractedly the meditation that is already free from distraction, without clinging or grasping.
Do not lose that state, and do not conjure anything in your mind.
Then abide in the field where there are no more pitfalls, mistakes, and deviations.
The one key point is to unmistakenly know what to cultivate (virtues) and what to abandon (nonvirtues).

11

Maintaining Awareness

Imagine that you are doing a meditation retreat for a few days or even a few weeks. You would create guidelines for the retreat, and a daily schedule would be part of that. The whole day would be divided into different meditation sessions, called *tün* in Tibetan, with breaks in between. The terms *meditation* and *post-meditation* are used to describe these different periods of time.

Usually, post-meditation denotes the period when one is no longer formally practicing meditation or doing any formal spiritual observances. This period occurs throughout the day, even during a meditation retreat. It is the time when you get up from the meditation cushion and officially end that meditation session. You may walk outside, start chopping vegetables, or briefly talk with a visitor. This is usually a time when our minds naturally get a little more relaxed in order to engage with the world.

Sometimes, meditative awareness can be lost during this time because we are not sitting in a meditation posture. Occasionally, our minds can completely wander away from awareness and revert to our usual state, which tends to be unconscious. We may get caught up in our thoughts or become enmeshed in very ordinary mental states.

This idea of meditation and post-meditation periods may not apply to most people in the world if they do not practice meditation, as they have no reference point for it. It is relevant only to those who practice meditation in their everyday life.

Individuals who are interested in meditation may need a daily formal meditation period where they block out other activities to focus solely on the practice, whether sitting on a cushion or in a chair. It doesn't have to be a long stretch of time; it can be as short as ten minutes.

Once there is an ongoing daily meditation period, then the concepts of meditation and post-meditation are much more relevant. When we get up from the meditation seat, the entire day becomes one long post-meditation period.

Now the question is, how do we maintain awareness, or the meditative state, while we are in action?

The Four Activities

Buddhist scriptures often categorize human activities quite simply, at a very basic level: eating, sleeping, going, and sitting. This way of summarizing all our activities reflects a humorous and humbling attitude toward human behavior. Usually, we think we are engaging in important endeavors that distinguish us from animals, whom we perceive as doing repetitive and insignificant behaviors. If you tell a human being that these four activities are all they are doing, it would be regarded as the ultimate affront to their ego. It feels like one is demoted to being an idle, unproductive being. Yet, in some ways, this is exactly what we are doing all the time. Whether we are wandering in the forest, going to the office to meet with VIPs to make a risky decision, strolling endlessly on a beach, or riding in a limousine, it is essentially the same activity: going. So these four categories encompass all that we do in this world.

The ultimate goal is to transcend the duality of meditation and post-meditation, reaching a point where one lives in awareness regardless of whether one is meditating or totally engaged in mundane activities. This experience can happen to us every now and then. But to truly live in that state of consciousness all the time requires a profound purification of all our mental habits. At the same time, it is an inspiring goal that we can all aim toward.

This state is described by many Dzogchen masters. For example, Shabkar, in his well-known book *The Flight of Garuda*, writes that when you reach such a state, you transcend what is spiritual and not spiritual, sacred and not sacred, meditation and post-meditation, or even breaking tantric precepts and maintaining them. You transcend all of these.

He also states that, at that point, all our physical movements can be regarded as mudras. Usually, mudras are sacred gestures performed in Tantric Buddhist ceremonies or the hand gestures of deities depicted in paintings and sculptures. These mudras are not just ordinary hand movements; they carry profound religious and sacred significance.

In the conventional sense, our physical movements, such as walking, sitting, and so on, are not considered mudras but just ordinary movements. For example, imagine that you are somewhere in Tibet. You may go to a temple, a monastery, or a sacred site to perform a circumambulation. This is called *korwa*, which is regarded as a holy observance. However, if you go to a market to shop or walk back and forth on the street, that is not usually considered a holy observance. But Shabkar says that for a Dzogchen yogi who is able to live in rigpa all the time, there is no longer any difference. To the yogi, it is all the same; whether they go to a sacred site to do circumambulation or go to town for something mundane, like buying a soda at a convenience store, their movement is considered korwa.

Shabkar goes on to say that for such a yogi, even eating and drinking is viewed as the highest offering. Offering is one of the holy observances that people practice in the East. People go to temples and show reverence by making offerings to the divine. In Tibetan, this is called *chöpa*. But Shabkar states that if you live in awareness all the time, even what we regard as a worldly activity like eating and drinking can be seen as a sacred performance—like offering. There is no difference between them.

The Dance of the Six Consciousnesses

Buddhist doctrines, such as Abhidharma, describe six consciousnesses, which are associated with the eye, ear, nose, tongue, body, and mind. In Dzogchen, we use these categories in regard to maintaining awareness while experiencing the inner and outer worlds through them.

When we wake up in the morning, we begin to engage with both the interior and exterior worlds. The interior world is made up of the thoughts, feelings, emotions, and moods that visit us without any deliberate invitation. One thing we can be sure of is that when we wake up, we don't need to do anything—our interior world is waiting for us. Sometimes, in that first moment of waking, we feel terrific, perhaps from having a deep sleep or because of the way the light shines through the window. Other times, we wake up and everything feels like drudgery for no apparent reason. Usually, we don't get stuck in that uninspiring feeling. It goes away on its own with an unbelievably simple remedy, such as just getting out of bed.

The exterior world is made up of all the outer stimuli, such as interactions with people, the taste and smell of food, the temperature we feel, the colors of the clothing people wear, the sounds of music or cars passing by, and so on. As this unbelievably rich and colorful world unfolds, we experience it through the lens of the six types of consciousness. These experiences are the very thing that gives us the sense of being alive right now.

In Dzogchen, one of the main practices, both during meditation and post-meditation, is not to get lost in the field of the six consciousnesses. This is not to say that we should completely block our senses and go into a sensory-deprived, one-dimensional mind. Instead, it means to welcome all the stimuli from within and without. At the same time, we don't reify them or let the mind get caught up in them. So there is no grasping or holding on to experiences either. We simply let them dance on their own as they appear and disappear.

This practice might not be challenging during sitting meditation, but it might be difficult during post-meditation. When we get up from the meditation cushion or start the day in general, we are living the raw and rich fullness of life. At that point, it is easy to get lost in the experience of the six consciousnesses. When that happens, we can easily get trapped in the snare of human emotions, such as attachment, aversion, attraction, repulsion, preferences, liking, and disliking. The matrix of duality becomes very intense, and so does our ego.

However, as we live life and welcome all its rich expressions, we can still maintain awareness and avoid being trapped by the experiences. Then there is an inner liberation, not by literally transcending or rejecting the world or life, nor by turning our attention away from those parts of life we feel we cannot resist. Instead, we can still live in the spirit of inner liberation in the middle of life with the intricate tapestry of emotions, passions, and everything else.

One time, during my trip to teach a meditation retreat in Austin, Texas, a group of friends took me to a huge restaurant filled with activity, lights, colors, music, and people. It was very tempting to go into an ordinary state of consciousness and be pulled by judgment, wanting, and grasping. It felt like being pulled out of oneself and being dragged into this wild, apparent, colorful display of the world around us. One of the people in the group was a poet and songwriter, and he began chanting in a low, Buddhist-like voice, "Appearances are distractions." When he said that, it was like the sound of a temple bell reminding my mind that I was about to get lost in the outside world. It was a reminder for all of us to come back to ourselves right away.

Dealing with Distraction

Post-meditation is a period when our practice can face challenges, sometimes even more than during formal meditation. One of the primary challenges is that we can easily be distracted by small things, which pull us back into the egoic, unconscious mind.

Maintaining Awareness

Certain things can easily trigger our reactivity and throw us into an unaware state, like being swept up by a huge tornado. All it takes is a single moment of losing one's awareness. Then a thought arises, we unconsciously jump on it, and we are carried into an unending virtual reality, either very fun or very dreadful. Then we react without any awareness.

This sad situation happens all the time because many people in the world live without much inner reflection, not looking into their minds to see how they are living internally. In other words, they do not examine the quality of their inner life. When the interior world is completely neglected, we live every day unconsciously with repetitive thoughts and emotions, holding on to mental patterns that cause unnecessary suffering. We close the door to the experience of pure joy, transcendence, and universal love, as they are not even in the equation of possibility.

Once we begin to look into the interior world, we see that attending to our inner life is as important as attending to our exterior life. This is reflected in the words of Socrates, who said, "An unexamined life is not worth living."

In this doha, Dudjom Lingpa reminds us not to be distracted. Being distracted means that we lose awareness and get caught up in our experiences. This can happen easily. One moment we are fully present, and the next moment, a thought arises, and we end up following it. That single moment can throw us into a wild world of mental drama or a long storyline.

Try to think of a time, either today, yesterday, or a few days ago, when you were completely lost in your mind and were suffering internally. Perhaps you were stuck with some storylines that caused you to feel unhappy, depressed, or scared. If you trace how that internal suffering began, you will find that its genesis was a single thought that arose in your mind, either a new thought or a recurring thought pattern. Because you were not in awareness at that moment, the thought proliferated and took over.

Now imagine that you were in awareness when that thought arose. Perhaps you could have witnessed it, and then it would dissolve on its own and not proliferate. Then you would not have gone through that inner agony.

The Power of Intention

There is a way that we can maintain rigpa, or awareness, in all our ordinary human activities. The secret is to set the intention each day when we wake up: to maintain rigpa, awareness, all the time throughout the day as the main priority. Once we set that intention, it leaves an imprint on our mind that will not easily be erased or lost in the mind's activities. That commitment can stay in our mind regardless of its focus throughout the day.

In general, our intention and aspiration often help us continue whatever journey we are on. This was understood by people of ancient times, so the Buddhist tradition uses many ceremonies to set intentions or hold commitments. It can be helpful to perform some ceremonies when we are part of a spiritual tradition, such as reciting sacred verses that encourage us to hold the commitment to live with awareness throughout the day.

In the old days in Tibet, quite a few meditators would get up in the morning and chant liturgies as a way to set their intention before going about their day. Then in the evening, before going to bed, they would meditate or recite liturgies to wrap up the day.

Maintaining Awareness

In the modern world, people are very comfortable writing words of their own resolution to align their hearts with such intentionality. Sometimes people share with me the words of resolution that they composed for their own hearts. I find them so beautiful and inspiring that I want to incorporate their words into my daily life.

Once we start the day with the power of intention, we will feel a kind of remembrance throughout the day to stay in rigpa. That remembrance can be regarded as our noble spiritual friend who gently reminds us to stay on the right course. In Buddhism, we take refuge in the sangha, or noble friendship. One of the main purposes of that refuge is to be in the company of someone who will always remind us of our highest purpose. So our intention or remembrance is like our inner sangha.

The power of that intention will direct our mind to be in awareness again and again. Then we can meet all situations not from the ego, which reacts out of fear, grasping, and aversion, but from a place that is spacious, free, and non-egoic.

Methods to Maintain Awareness

Even though rigpa is beyond any doing and is the uncontrived, natural state of mind as it is, we may need to remind ourselves not to be distracted and to be present as much as possible. So there are also practical methods we can apply to drop into rigpa when we lose touch with it.

For example, we might use the technique of pausing every now and then, even for a few seconds, to disrupt the continuation of unconscious mental chatter. Without applying any further technique, we can pause, disentangle ourselves from our thoughts, and drop into awareness as if we are having a fresh start. I call this a "sacred pause."

Sometimes that pause can be an inquiry where we ask ourselves, "What is the state of my mind right now?" With that question, our mind suddenly stops being on the treadmill of conceptual activities for a moment. Then awareness emerges immediately through which we see exactly where our mind is—whether we are in awareness or completely lost in thought. The point is not to reward ourselves for being present or to judge ourselves for losing awareness. It is simply about returning to awareness.

Another method to return to awareness is to recite certain syllables that can help us break a state of unawareness, such as exclaiming "PHAD." When the continuation of such unawareness suddenly stops, there is an inner space where we can drop into awareness. From then on, we don't need to do anything to reach a higher state of meditation or awareness. Now we are in rigpa.

One time, Dza Patrul Rinpoche, one of the great Dzogchen masters, was practicing meditation in a beautiful forest called Ari Nak in the Golok region of Eastern Tibet. It was said that people saw him walking in the forest by himself, exclaiming "Ha ha ha!" Most likely, he used that sound to be alert, to shock his thinking mind, and become completely immersed in a state of pure, present, naked awareness.

The Fruits of Continuous Practice

As we continue to maintain awareness in our everyday life, even if a negative thought arises, we will remember not to indulge in it. As we continue such practice, our mind will gradually develop the skill to deal with our thoughts and experiences. We will find we are less and less caught up in our mind. This can bring about a true sense of well-being in our life. Our quality of life will keep improving as our state of mind improves.

It's like learning to drive a car. In the beginning, you may have to practice driving with someone, but eventually you can drive on your own without needing anyone's presence. But there may be a period when you feel a little insecure and have to pay attention all the time, learning how to control the car. After a while, you may not need as much effort to control the car. Your body will do everything automatically, even though you are fully aware of your surroundings at every moment. You can feel relaxed, sing a song, and look around, making driving really enjoyable.

In the same way, through the power of our ongoing practice, there comes a point when we don't have to constantly remind ourselves to be in awareness in daily life. We may feel that awareness has become the default mode of our mind. Many negative patterns may be gone, and there is less fuel for reactivity. A lot of situations that used to bother us no longer do. What a relief that is! Our inner joy will increase without needing any effort to cultivate it.

Then we feel we are experiencing what we call "life," not from our egoic state of mind but from a state of mind that we can call rigpa—or any name, such as an open heart or pure love.

Commitment to Dzogchen

The spiritual awakening of the Dzogchen masters of the past is undoubtedly a testimony to the power of Dzogchen practice. We cannot even argue about it. Although many beautiful spiritual experiences arise, to truly change our life so that it is rooted in spiritual awakening often requires a commitment to Dzogchen practice. Sometimes it is easy to be satisfied with some experiences and then let go of the practice. Or we might continue to practice periodically only when we are in the mood to do it. Another possibility is that even though we are spiritual and sincere, we can become a spiritual hungry ghost, always chasing more practices and more theories, and lose our focus on Dzogchen practice itself.

The renowned fourth Dodrupchen Rinpoche lived most of his life in Sikkim. One time, he returned to his hometown in Eastern Tibet. It was announced that he would give *abhisheka*, or "tantric initiation," at his monastery there. Dodrupchen was a revered lama, and his presence in Eastern Tibet was very rare, so many people went there to receive the abhisheka as a precious opportunity.

At that time, some of Khenpo Munsel's disciples asked him whether they should attend. Khenpo Munsel responded by saying, "I taught you everything you need to know." Then he quoted a famous Tibetan expression:

Instead of wearing out your shoes by running around,
wear out your meditation cushion by sitting on it.

Khenpo Munsel was not indicating that Dodrupchen's initiation was unimportant. He was trying to say that they should focus on the Dzogchen practice that they already know.

This is how we can bring about authentic transformation in our lives. With an unwavering commitment to Dzogchen practice, someday we may join the circle of truly inspiring Dzogchen masters of the past. Then our lives may inspire others to wake up.

Maintaining Awareness

Beyond Meditation and Post-Meditation

Even though in many moments, we may drift away from awareness, the Dzogchen masters say that we can arrive at a point when the demarcation between meditation and post-meditation is transcended and live in awareness almost all the time. This is a moment when our mind has shed much of its egoic, habitual patterns, so there is not a big force that drags us into unawareness.

We should not rule out such a possibility. For someone like myself, living in rigpa all the time feels like an impossible task. But when I think of certain individuals, it opens my mind to such a possibility. There are people I have met in my lifetime who strike me as having the capacity to live in rigpa even in ordinary interactions with others.

One of them is Lama Garwang. It is not that he verbally claimed this was his state, but it is my impression. Seeing the way he carried himself and learning about how he dealt with difficult situations convinced me that he is someone who lived in such an awakened state of consciousness.

He is not the only one. I also had the good fortune to be around other authentic Dzogchen masters, and I felt extremely comfortable in their presence. There is a common phenomenon one experiences when around them, as far as my perception is concerned: a sense of being accepted, and the ability to be who I am without being judged. Most likely, my feeling of being so carefree around them is because it seemed they interacted with me not from their ego but from being totally grounded in rigpa and embodying an open heart.

I grew up in a Tibetan culture that is ancient, traditional, and infused with Buddhism. Sacred devotion is all-pervasive in the consciousness of the Tibetan people. Because of that, I myself had very strong devotion toward the Buddhist archetypes of buddhas and bodhisattvas, such as Tara and Avalokiteshvara. My grandparents, whom I regard as my first spiritual teachers, always chanted the names of both of these buddhas, which enhanced my devotion to them. I always felt that Tara and Avalokiteshvara were buddhas who totally accepted me as I am, with all my imperfections. I realized that I had been longing for that kind of acceptance since I was young. I was not seeking a powerful figure who praised me but pure acceptance without any judgment.

This is not just my own experience; many people are longing for this as well. In many ways, my grandparents gave me that total love. Also, when I sat in the presence of Dzogchen masters, I felt I was in the presence of Tara and Avalokiteshvara, completely accepted as I am, without needing to be someone else.

Such encounters are precious and undoubtedly have a healing impact on us. I feel that these Dzogchen masters were shining examples of how we can relate to each other from the highest state of consciousness. When we relate to each other from such awareness, we not only find a sense of harmony, ease, and trust with others but we also heal the wounds that may be hidden in our psyche.

12

Engaging with Life

Many people feel that their mind is cleansed and their heart is open after a long period of meditation. They often feel they are able to let go of a lot of pain in their heart along with unhealthy, destructive concepts and opinions. They feel an opening and transformation at an energetic, psychosomatic level. They are also able to see the world and everyone in it through a different lens of their consciousness, one that recognizes the beauty and wonder in all things that exist.

One time, a group of us were coming back from a meditation retreat, feeling happy and commenting on how nice everything was that we saw along the road, including houses and buildings. Then one of them told me they coined a term a long time ago called the "nice-neighborhood syndrome." I asked what the story was behind that. They said that once some of them did a weeklong meditation retreat, and when they came out, one of them kept saying, "Oh, this is such a nice neighborhood." And then at the next area, the same person said it again, "Oh, this is such a nice neighborhood." She was seeing everything through an openhearted consciousness that came from being immersed in meditation.

But the truth is that these experiences don't last long because they are often interrupted by the smallest challenges that revive our habitual patterns. Even with such a powerful awakening and purification of the mind, many of our habitual patterns do not go away overnight. Otherwise, all we would need is an extraordinary inner epiphany, and we would be enlightened immediately. All the wise meditators of the past are very familiar with this phenomenon of habitual patterns returning again and again. It is like cutting some of the weeds in your backyard. You think they are uprooted, but to your surprise, they grow back again. This is why it is important to commit to live in rigpa in all situations.

Beyond Techniques

So the question is, how do we stay in rigpa even in ordinary environments? The idea is challenging, but when it comes down to the method, it is simple. It can be so simple that it may be hard to believe.

There are also numerous methods and disciplines that can help us, as we already mentioned. For example, some Dzogchen texts say you should exclaim syllables throughout the day to return to rigpa. On the other hand, it may not be practical to apply these methods in everyday life. Imagine you are standing in line at the grocery store and start exclaiming some syllables—people around you may get irritated or worse. It would be weird in any situation, whether you are having dinner with someone, or in a movie theater, or at an airport. If you are by yourself or in a retreat, no problem. But otherwise, exclaiming syllables may not only be impractical but it may also draw the wrong kind of attention from other people.

Engaging with Life

In the end, we can drop all the complex methods and disciplines. Maybe that is what we are supposed to aim toward. The whole thing may sound quite paradoxical—we learn all these methods so we can reach a place where we are no longer dependent on them.

Whether you use a technique or not, the point is simply to remember to come back to rigpa. Remembering is the ultimate method, the secret method. In some ways, it is not really a method. For most people, we need to go through a period of daily training where we intentionally do sitting meditation, either in retreat or everyday life, and then commit to maintaining awareness throughout the day. This is how most people need to train their mind to anchor itself in a state that is not ruled by unawareness.

Then at some point, after practicing for a while, each day we are able to remember to maintain awareness. Such ability would not be contingent on place or situation. We could be standing at a very ordinary place, like a gas station, or engaging in the most mundane activity, like doing the laundry, or meeting with some unpleasant situation. We will clearly see a huge difference between leading our life from the egoic state of mind versus from awareness. The difference is that we experience so much pain and suffering when our life operates from the ego, and we find an abundance of joy when our life rests on the ground of awareness. It is a nonmaterial reward, so our whole being is naturally drawn to live in that freedom. Our heart will be so in love with that freedom, it will not be tempted to return to unawareness.

The Mind's Capacity for Freedom

Our mind has the extraordinary potential to go beyond all the internal limits constructed by our ego. Sometimes, we might be stuck with a certain state of mind, and it can be difficult to imagine that we can get beyond it. When we are lost in suffering, it is hard to imagine that we can experience bliss. When we are trapped by anger and hatred, it is hard to imagine that we can experience love. When we are completely identified with the personal self, it is hard to imagine that we can transcend it.

Yet Dzogchen points out that the very nature of our mind is already the dharmakaya, the ultimate Buddha. Therefore, we need to harbor the faith and trust in our innate capacity to actualize what we may consider the highest level, or the very peak, of consciousness, whether we call that enlightenment, universal love, or something else.

The mind has the capacity to break its falsely constructed boundaries and expand itself infinitely so that it can love everyone and experience equilibrium in all situations. Even in the midst of painful and sometimes challenging situations, our mind has the potential to experience stillness, peace, and pure unconditional joy.

Viktor Frankl—a holocaust survivor and author of *Man's Search for Meaning*—personally went through and was surrounded by unimaginable human suffering during his time in a concentration camp. He gained profound insight from his time there, which he articulated like this:

> Everything can be taken from a man but one thing: the last of the human freedoms—to choose one's attitude in any given set of circumstances, to choose one's own way.*

---

* Viktor E. Frankl, *Man's Search for Meaning* (Beacon Press, 2006), 66.

He found that when we are able to change our attitude, we won't lose dignity even in the harshest situations. His wisdom is a powerful testimony that this human mind has so much potential that we can even find freedom in the most difficult circumstances by such a shift.

Effortless Introspection

One of the most powerful yet not complex ways to actualize the mind's spiritual potential is a practice called *samprajnana* (introspection).

There are two ways of practicing samprajnana. One is based on deliberate effort to watch your mind all the time with a lot of concentration, noticing what is happening in your mind. This type of introspection is taught in various Buddhist traditions. In this method, if you find some negative thoughts arise, you try to push them away, separate yourself from them, or practice what is called an "antidote." This can be very useful for many people at a certain stage of their spiritual path. For example, if you are feeling hatred, then you may meditate on compassion to counteract it.

This method is like having an overactive GPS that constantly narrates everything that is happening—the houses you pass by, the potholes on the road, and the turns you don't take. It could be helpful, but there is a point where it becomes quite annoying.

Then there is a Dzogchen way of practicing samprajnana, which you might call "effortless introspection." Or we might like to call it something like "mindfulness beyond mindfulness." Essentially, it is effortless. We don't always have to watch what is happening in our mind with such intensity: "Uh-oh. Another negative thought. I don't like what is happening in my mind. Oh, this is not good. Oh, now I'm feeling compassion for someone. How spiritual I am . . ." and so forth.

Instead of a superego that is continuously monitoring all our internal events, the Dzogchen way is to practice effortless, nonjudgmental introspection. We don't constantly watch our mind and judge ourselves. Instead, there is a sense of a totally carefree awareness, yet we are not living unconsciously. In that awareness, we are not operating in a mindless mode but are fully aware of what is happening in our mind.

At the same time, we are no longer lost in our experiences. Our mind is free, no matter what we are going through in that moment . . . joy, sadness, elation, anxiety. The very core of our being is no longer contracted. Eventually, the energetic glue between ourselves and negative mental patterns wears out, and many of them may go away completely. We may see that deep-seated mental patterns or certain fears that stultify us may disappear without any residue.

Then even though many ordinary human challenges and experiences accompany us in everyday life, we feel we can dance with them, and we have enough awareness that we don't allow ourselves to be trapped by them. This free, open introspection can purify all our negative mental patterns and bring about joy, healing, and a sense of well-being in our lives. We feel we return to our true home, our original nature.

Seeing Everything as the Display of Awareness

When we are fully present with our experience, we can welcome all our thoughts and emotions with the radical attitude that whatever is happening inside is neither good nor bad. Such a radical attitude is taught in Dzogchen as the notion that we can embrace everything that pops up in our life as a miraculous display of awareness, *rigpé rol tsal*. This does not only refer to internal experiences; all external events that occur in our everyday life are also welcomed from this point of view. To live each day from this perspective fundamentally replaces our old dualistic way of looking at things with a totally liberating, nondual lens through which we can see reality in a very different light.

In our dualistic consciousness, we tend to perceive everything that is happening as good or bad, favorable or unfavorable, with a powerful illusion that we are a separate self interacting with a reality outside. Then we react and get caught up in attachment, aversion, fear, irritation, and so on. All of these internal ups and downs are often caused by our own perception rather than the nature of reality itself.

Seeing everything as a display of rigpa, or awareness, has a very profound philosophical meaning. It is not just some kind of nice-sounding phrase to use as a spiritual pacifier. It is not just a mantra or prayer that we recite when we feel that we need to calm our mind or anchor ourselves in equilibrium; this phrase should not be regarded as a sacred platitude.

Seeing everything as a display of awareness does not mean that we lack discrimination and let everything happen without any response. This notion should be held with careful understanding. Our ego can easily hijack such an idea and lead us to become passive, deny reality, or lead us into a cozy mental bubble of irresponsibility. Often people can misunderstand and even misuse these profound spiritual teachings to feed some part of the ego. Yet these teachings can have a truly liberating impact when we understand them.

To see everything as a display of rigpa means to welcome all situations from a non-egoic state of consciousness at the same time that we take right action in the context of any specific situation. Imagine that you see someone in trouble in front of you. You don't just sit there, not doing anything, saying, "It is all a display of awareness." Instead, if you truly understand what that teaching means, you will be able to have compassion, sympathy, and take action to help the person.

When we are able to apply this wisdom in real situations in our lives, instead of becoming emotionally aloof, our hearts will open, and we will have an even greater level of compassion and altruism in relation to the world.

All Experiences Self-Liberate

The Dzogchen way does not mean that we are always experiencing intoxicating, noble feelings, such as wanting to help the world, having compassion, or being blissed out, which are, of course, all good. It doesn't really matter what we experience—it is all *rigpé rol tsal*.

This attitude is fundamentally openhearted and nonjudgmental. It allows us to welcome whatever arises in our mind—the spiritual as well as the mundane—as the miraculous display of rigpa. Then we feel we are not pushed by the impulse to hold on to them, nor have the desire to transcend them. We don't even attempt to liberate our own mind.

This is where the idea of self-liberation comes into being. For example, fear liberates on its own. Isn't that nice? Usually we think, "I have to liberate myself from fear." But in this case, fear liberates on its own without using any effort to change it or transcend it. Anger liberates on its own. So too jealousy or any other negative emotion because the true nature of all of them is the same as the true nature of love. The true nature of everything is the same. It's—we have no one word for it—it is the sacred, it is the ineffable, it is the miraculous display of awareness. It is the ultimate purity.

As an example, think about two utterly different things—one could be your golden ring, which is very precious as well as priceless. Then imagine another object that you regard as worthless, like all the stuff in your trash can. According to the convention that we humans hold as a consensus, there is no comparison between them. One is precious and beautiful, and the other is worthless and ready to be thrown out.

But from a cosmic point of view, there is not a big difference between them at the fundamental level of their makeup. All we need to do is bring a little astrophysics into this equation. Then we see that both of these objects are made of similar substances that can be traced back to stardust. There is neither good nor bad stardust.

It is not that we can't have anger. I think sometimes anger is necessary. But in this practice, we don't hold on to anger. In Tibetan culture, there is a famous proverb that says, "An enlightened mind can get angry, but it does not hold on to it." This reminds us that anger or any other human experience is natural.

So the enlightened mind is not some kind of sublime spiritual mind that is devoid of all these very raw human experiences. Not at all. The only difference between an enlightened mind and a deluded, confused mind is that the enlightened mind does not hold on to anything.

We also may have unconscious beliefs about what it means to be enlightened. Maybe we think that it means to live in some kind of perfect consciousness that is always full of love and compassion, always filled with joy, and we never experience these very ordinary, raw human emotions like anger or jealousy. But we have to let go of that idea.

Instead, according to Dzogchen, all we need to do is simply carry out this effortless introspection, knowing what is happening in the moment. Then, sometimes when we experience very ordinary thoughts and other human emotions, we should recognize them but know that we don't have to follow them. We don't have to indulge in them. That's all we need to do. As long as we are able to carry out effortless introspection, then we can say we are embodying and living Dzogchen in everyday life.

The Challenges of Illness and Death

Such a radical perspective can be applied in the face of very challenging situations in our lives, including things that may shake us to the core. This was the central practice of Dzogchen masters of the past. As Longchenpa said,

> For indeed, all that manifests, all that occurs, every fault and every quality are but the display of awareness, nothing else. When one is well, this is the display of awareness; when one is unhappy, this too is awareness; when one is ill, this is awareness; when one is joyful, this also is awareness. Apart from awareness, there is simply nothing.

For example, when the time of death approached some of the ancient Dzogchen masters, it is said that their consciousness was not shaken by fear of dying. Instead, they saw that even death is an illusion. They saw the whole last stage of life as a beautiful journey to the supreme source, or the *dharmadhatu*, instead of being scared or thinking that they were reaching a morbid extinction of existence. In the same way, some Dzogchen masters were able to apply this attitude to other challenging situations, such as loss, illness, and old age.

In general, we all know that illness is not fun to experience. Of course, that's true if we are seriously sick with some painful terminal illness. But even just having a cold can sometimes bring us down. Many illnesses bring pain and if not pain, definitely physical discomfort. Illness is not totally mental. It is a pure physical experience, and we cannot pretend it is not happening.

At the same time, there is a way we can work with illness. Having a nondual perspective allows us to let go of the usual stories that we have about illness and discomfort. Our usual reactions to physical discomfort create a very strong physical and emotional resistance to what we are experiencing, which can intensify the level of suffering. Jigme Lingpa wrote an entire doha on how to work with illness, in which he said,

> Do not carry illness into your mind.
> Instead, relax your awareness onto illness.

He is saying we should not identify with illness. Our mind habitually tends to identify with illness unless that default mode is disrupted. Usually when we are sick, a narrative happens—"I am sick, this is terrible, I don't like what I am experiencing, I can't do this and that."

Many people don't have the training to experience physical discomfort with nonreactive awareness. But as we said, when we feel discomfort or pain, the practice is to not identify with that pain or go into habitual modes of resistance, but instead to be with the physical experience in open, all-embracing awareness. If we are able to do this, we may not suffer too much. Even the level of pain can be reduced. As Machig Labdron wrote, "Don't identify illness as illness." In today's world, not just individual meditators but a variety of institutions, such as hospitals, are teaching some form of Buddhist meditation to work with pain. They are finding positive results, and many people are benefiting from it.

Dzogchen: A Source of Healing

In today's culture, there is so much talk about trauma as well as post-traumatic stress disorder (PTSD). People are traumatized by a variety of circumstances: being in a war zone, being abused or neglected, or dealing with a tragic circumstance.

Trauma is also a manifestation of what happened to us and how we respond to it. For example, I knew some of the Dzogchen masters in our time who went through horrific situations, such as being jailed for years because of religious persecution. The jails included hard physical labor, very little food, and all kinds of mistreatment.

When these Dzogchen masters came out of jail, rather than being angry, broken souls who became alcoholics, they shocked everyone by their dignity and wisdom. They radiated a presence of grace and benevolence. They did not demonstrate any signs of PTSD. This is quite incredible. It is not that they were born as some superhuman beings, but they applied the radical Dzogchen attitudes. Their minds were free all along and didn't get lost in anger and hopelessness.

These masters are a living testimony to the power of the Dzogchen teachings and their practicality. Today, in this wild world, our hearts can be easily wounded, and our minds can become so confused. Therefore, the Dzogchen teachings can be a healing medicine that will bring ease and freedom to our hearts and minds.

A Foundation of Ethics

Dudjom Lingpa's doha echoes the Dzogchen masters of the past, such as Padmasambhava, who taught that no matter how advanced our spiritual practice might be, in the end, we should always remember not to be reckless in our behavior. Therefore, ethics is the foundation of all Buddhist practices, including Dzogchen.

Without the framework of ethics in our spirituality, it is incomplete and it may not take us anywhere in terms of authentic awakening or even personal transformation. Our spirituality can be hijacked by ego, self-interest, ulterior motives, self-deception, and narcissism. The practice of ethics brings goodness into our lives as well as goodness in our relationships between ourselves and the world.

What is ethics? Sometimes it refers to understanding the line between wholesome and unwholesome actions—cultivating wholesome actions, and refraining from unwholesome actions. Sometimes ethics is not only what we do but the state of mind that we cultivate.

The Buddhist system of ethics is very complex because the definition of ethics varies according to the different systems of practices and philosophies. Yet there is one universal system of ethics agreed upon by all the systems, which is *ahimsa* in Sanskrit, or "nonviolence." It means refraining from harming others either directly or indirectly. Buddhist ethics is not exclusively human-centric, so nonviolence is exercised not just toward people but toward all living beings, with not one single species excluded, no matter how insignificant or different it is from humans.

There is a danger, especially when people get into nondual advanced spiritual practices. They may ignore the importance of ethics or may be "barking up the wrong tree," thinking that the higher teachings literally transcend the system of ethics. It gives the ego a self-fulfilling fantasy that one can enjoy the bliss of enlightenment even while doing whatever one wants without any restraint, letting one's primitive impulses be unhinged. Such a misunderstanding can eventually lead us to pitfalls, where we end up disregarding the law of karma, and ethics is no longer part of our spirituality. This can be very dangerous and can lead to both philosophical and behavioral disasters.

In order to prevent such misadventures, Dudjom Lingpa reminds us that while we are practicing Dzogchen, we should always make sure we are following the fundamental guidelines of ethics.

Cultivating Virtue and Abandoning Nonvirtue

Ethics could be categorized into two: what to cultivate and what to refrain from. The first is what we regard as virtue, or wholesome action. This comes down to one single principle—to benefit others. In Tibetan, it is called *zhenpen*. The second one—what to refrain from—is harming others, or in Tibetan, *zhennö*.

When we think of harming others, we should not just associate it with hurting someone physically or causing serious emotional abuse. There are so many subtle ways we can hurt other people unless we bring intentional reflection to what we do and say. Even the words we use are extremely important. When we call people names based on their physical characteristics, race, religion, or lifestyle, even if we don't have a bad intention, such words can be tainted by collective phobia and discrimination against others. They can be perceived as different, undesirable, or less than us, and so forth.

In Tibetan culture, a society completely imbued with Buddhist principles, people are encouraged to incorporate these two aspects of ethics into everyday life. Most people in Tibetan society have an idea of Buddhist ethics, but individuals may vary in how much they live by it. There are even certain observances where you practice ethics in relation to animals. For example, many Tibetan people are very careful about harming other living beings, such as animals and insects, and, of course, humans.

The great master Patrul Rinpoche is known for practicing ethics and for embodying the phrase spoken by Padmasambhava:

One's view should be as high as the sky.
Yet one's conduct should be as fine as flour.

It is said that Patrul Rinpoche was so concerned with the well-being of animals that he felt that riding horses was a form of animal abuse, and he vowed not to ride horses. During his lifetime, he walked on foot all the time, which was a huge sacrifice. In those days, riding a horse was a means of transportation in Tibet, like cars are today.

Anam Chatralwa, who was one of the earliest disciples of Dudjom Lingpa, was a lifelong hermit, and he vowed at some point not to eat meat nor wear any animal products for clothes. He only wore quilt clothes, mainly made out of sheep wool, and lived in a tent his whole life, practicing meditation in the higher altitudes of the Himalayas. This was a huge sacrifice since in those days, most people wore animal products like yak and sheep skin, the main material for clothing in many parts of Tibet. His way of life did not come from an outdated religious doctrine but from one principle: not to harm others.

Ethics as a Cornerstone of Life

Having a moral ethic in your mind can become a little passive, like having a conscience but not acting on it. It can become a form of moral inertia. Tibetan society has practices that keep our psyche from atrophying in this inertia, such as going into the mountains and feeding ant colonies. Also, in the old days, some trails were covered with rocks, and people would spend the whole day there, removing the rocks so that people and animals could move with ease. People did that as a religious practice.

Ethics is not just a cultural or religious matter. It should be held as the very foundation of our spiritual practice. It can also bring about dignity and inner happiness to oneself. Furthermore, human society may not even survive at all without ethics as the cornerstone of our lives.

Human beings are very complex creatures. Sometimes a contradiction happens inside us—there is the desire to be good but at the same time, powerful forces and impulses lead us to do unwholesome deeds. We may feel these two forces fighting with each other. Yet in the end, we have the ability to decide which force we want to side with.

No doubt there is an innate aspiration in human beings to strive to be a good person, regardless of whether they are actually living in accordance with their high ideals. In our hearts, we often find so much goodness, such as altruism, our desire to help others, and our wish to live life in accordance with noble principles. This is why, collectively, we honor certain individuals as heroes and heroines who embody virtue, not because of their personal power, wealth, or physical prowess.

How to Practice Ethics

The way we practice ethics should not just be based on some ancient books that dictate a do-and-don't list. Many holy scriptures that have been a moral manual are outdated or derived from primitive societies, according to the standards of today's world.

The way to practice ethics is to look inside and see the powerful forces that motivate us to engage with unwholesome deeds. It could be greed, unhealthy desire, jealousy, hatred, anger, or any of the negative forces. Ultimately, all our actions come from our motives or impulses. Without acknowledging or working with these forces, we may outwardly pretend to follow a good example—like a good sheep in the human herd—but the roots of our negative actions haven't been purified.

This is why some Buddhist masters defined the line between *kushala* (virtue) and *akushala* (nonvirtue) as not just the action but the motivation behind the action. This seems to be a more holistic and logical way to define true ethics in our everyday life. As Nagarjuna said,

These three—greed, hatred, and ignorance—
actions done through them is akushala.
Free from greed, hatred, and ignorance—
actions done that way is kushala.

Even though human beings sometimes do things that are not only uninspiring but also destructive to themselves and others, this is not because human nature is intrinsically bad. We are extremely flexible and can choose to go low or go high. We can become noble, whether or not society gives us a crown for it. In fact, it could be better if no one gives recognition to our nobility.

Some Buddhist masters completely let go of attachment to the recognition of their holiness. For them, practicing ethics was not to gain popularity or to become loved by the masses but for their own inner evolution and the joy of it. That was so much their main focus that sometimes they did things that almost appeared to be a bit crazy or counterintuitive. It was as if they wanted to show their imperfections to others.

Geshe Ben was a famous Buddhist master in Tibet as well as a legendary cultural icon. People tell anecdotes about him even today as a source of both amusement and inspiration. He was known for being very honest with himself as well as a paragon of virtues.

Once, he came down from his hermitage to perform a ceremony for a family. At some point, everyone from the family was outside, and he saw a burlap sack of tea hanging from a pillar. He realized that he was out of tea in his hermitage. So he got up and started taking some of the tea from the sack. Suddenly, he was aware of what he was doing. He grabbed one of his hands with the other hand and shouted loudly, "Everyone, come here! I caught the thief."

Everyone rushed back and saw that Geshe Ben had one hand in the sack of tea, and the other hand was holding on to that hand.

The Joy of Virtue

There is also joy from not harming others and benefiting others, because our true nature is intrinsically good. When we follow universal ethical lines, our heart is more and more full, and we experience pure joy that cannot be found from material gain or sensual pleasures.

A Harvard Business School experiment gave students five dollars or twenty dollars to spend either on themselves or others. The researchers found that people who spent the money on themselves weren't happier, but people who spent it on others were. The researchers said, "The amount of money, five dollars or twenty dollars, didn't matter. It was only how people spent it that made them happier."

This is an example of the intrinsic goodness in our hearts as human beings, and when we do good things in the world, our hearts' deeper needs are fulfilled. This results in a nonmaterial joy.

Ethics is both the state of our mind as well as being relational. It often involves what we do as well as how we relate to the world and other beings around us. Therefore, we cannot have true virtue or ethics if we don't bring ethical principles into our relationships with others.

True ethics is not just about following some old scriptures nor adhering to a behavior code dictated by any given society. Its roots—empathy and compassion—lie in each of us. When these two are lacking in us, we are prone to being very self-centered and have little reservation about causing harm to others. Empathy is a virtue, without which we are morally bankrupt. We can be extremely wealthy, basking in worldly glory, but without empathy, we are morally bankrupt.

Once again, the most important part of practicing ethics is to become aware of our inner dark forces and not give into them, no matter how tempting or irresistible they may be. We don't have to declare a sacred spiritual war against our inner dark forces. They don't go away easily, but when they occur, we don't need to take them personally. Everyone has dark forces, too. All we need to do is be aware of them and learn not to allow them to take over.

With such practice, eventually these forces have less and less of a grip on us. Then we find ourselves living in accordance with our higher principles, which often results in a sense of dignity and fulfillment.

May It Be Auspicious

སྤྱང་དྲེད་པོ་བདུད་འཇོམས་རྡོ་རྗེས་དགེ་མ་ཆོས་མཚོས་དོར་
འབོས་ཕུག་མཁའ་འགྲོའི་འདུ་ཁང་དུ་བྲིས། །དགེའོ། །

The stubborn beggar Dudjom Dorje wrote these words at the request of the nun named Chötsho at the Dakini Gathering Hall Cave of Dröpuk. May it be auspicious.

13

Kyor Jung: Reviewing the Teachings

It is typical in the Tibetan Buddhist tradition for students to gather after a teaching to review what they have learned. The term for reviewing the teachings is *kyor jung* in Tibetan. In that spirit, in this chapter, we will revisit what we talked about throughout the book, using different language and analogies, and expanding some methods.

The Root of Suffering

Dzogchen masters state that enlightenment does not come into being by transcending existence but by embracing it. This is quite radical because many spiritual traditions encourage people to transcend existence, responding to our longing to be free from the endless drudgery and messiness of life. Of course, there are countless moments where we are content, happy, and feel lucky to be alive. We have a sense that it was right to be born in this world. It could be special moments, like walking on the beach barefoot after a wonderful meal, or attending a graduation ceremony of a beloved family member, or the moment you finish a big project you have been working on, and so forth.

But on the other hand, many people feel it is hard to be a human being. Life comes with lots of hardships and problems—conflicts with people, health issues, financial struggles, or even boredom. While we hold on to life, there is also a part of us that wants to transcend it completely.

Dzogchen teaches that we can find freedom in the heart of existence without transcending it, because the problem is not existence nor life itself. It points out that the very root of suffering lies in our consciousness and not outside of it. Existence is fine as it is. That's good news, isn't it? That means we don't have to solve any problems from outside. We can cut through the very root of suffering in our consciousness.

Dzogchen points out that the root of suffering is not only in our consciousness, but it is also very simple. Unbelievably simple, and something we can discover right now: When consciousness gets lost in its own experiences, suffering begins.

Therefore, Dzogchen teaches that the very root of human suffering is a form of forgetfulness, which is a state where our consciousness is lost in its own experiences, the experience of the six consciousnesses: sight, sound, touch, taste, smell, and thoughts. When that unawareness happens, then suffering starts. Suffering doesn't need any other external factor—that's all it needs for it to emerge.

Let's talk about thoughts as an example. If consciousness is like an ocean, thoughts are like its waves. We don't have to do much to make them happen. They arise the way waves on the ocean arise—on their own. So thoughts are just an experience of consciousness. Then our mind can be lost in thoughts, not knowing that thought is an experience of its own consciousness. When we get lost in our thoughts, we can suffer; we can feel that our heart closes down right there, especially with negative thoughts.

Then our consciousness can experience aversion or fear or other negative forms of emotions. When we don't remember that all these are just experiences of our own consciousness, we can be lost in them, and then suffering begins. We can easily be lost in attachment and grasping, not realizing that these are simply experiences of consciousness itself. Then once again, suffering begins. This could happen even if you are living in the most idyllic sphere of the cosmos.

But if we have the ability to stay in awareness while we are experiencing everything and not let our consciousness get lost in experiences, then we can be free right there. We can be quite happy, regardless of what we are going through. We could be in a very difficult situation, or we could be in a really unpleasant environment, yet still we can be free and happy.

Be Present!

So the question is, how can we stop consciousness from being trapped and lost in its experiences? The remedy is very simple: it is present awareness. Present awareness can sometimes be very sublime and sometimes very ordinary. The way to be in present awareness can be through sacred practices, such as a mantra or visualization.

When you work with mantras and visualizations, you can experience that your consciousness is no longer lost—your consciousness is awakened in that very moment. It is no longer lost in aversion, attachment, fear, fantasy, thoughts. It is no longer trapped in all these experiences and sense perceptions. Of course, reciting a mantra can be done unconsciously, and it becomes another compulsion. But it can be used as a powerful method to return to present awareness.

When I think of my guru, Lama Tsurlo, he didn't sit in silence most of the time. He was always chanting mantras. He recited the mantra of wrathful Padmasambhava four hundred million times during his life. This was his main spiritual practice. And I always felt that every time he chanted the mantra, he was returning to awareness again and again.

Of course, you have to chant the mantra with awareness. We can chant the mantra unconsciously, and there are stories about people chanting mantras yet nothing happened to their consciousness. But somebody like Lama Tsurlo chanted the mantra with total awareness. I believe from the depth of my being that he didn't chant it as a mindless incantation but as a way to anchor in rigpa.

A Colloquial Mantra

In my tradition, one of the methods we use to disrupt the process of consciousness being lost in the self—lost in experiences of fear, aversion, attraction, desire, fantasy, or appearance—is to chant the name of Padmasambhava, Avalokiteshvara, or an enlightened being.

Sometimes, we even say an informal or colloquial mantra. In my culture, when we have some struggles in our life or go through fear or doubt, we very naturally say, "Oh, Tara, pay attention to me." Or, "Oh, Padmasambhava, be aware of me." We also call upon our gurus. We say, "Oh, Dudjom Lingpa, pay attention to me. May you be aware of me." I call these colloquial mantras since they are not really formal mantras.

Kyor Jung: Reviewing the Teachings

I have known some wonderful Tibetan lamas who, while walking outside, would say "Padmasambhava, be aware of me" whenever they saw something very attractive or enticing, such as delicious food. I was very curious why they would do this. Tibetans don't usually say such a prayer when they see something exquisite, but if they go through some difficulty or trip over something, they might sometimes say, "Oh, Padmasambhava, pay attention to me." But these lamas would sometimes call on Padmasambhava when they saw something utterly enticing.

My speculation is that they were calling on the guru so that they would not get lost in desire. That's my "pop psychoanalysis" of them. They were praying so they would not be lost in the senses.

As we quoted in the opening of this book, the Fifth Dalai Lama said that the guru, Padmasambhava, is our own awareness. When we call upon the guru, actually we are simply returning to our own awareness. We are invoking our own awareness, and therefore when we chant mantras, we feel present again, coming back to ourself. We are no longer lost or caught up in our experiences, either thoughts, fantasies, perceptions, or even external appearances. We feel that we are fully present again.

Breath and Sensations

Another more spontaneous way to be fully present in the midst of all our activities—when we feel consciousness is getting lost in experiences—is to feel sensations in our body. We can always feel sensations in our body if we direct our attention to them, no matter what we are doing. We can feel the sensation in our feet or the breath.

Suddenly paying attention to the breath in order to disrupt consciousness from descending into unawareness is a powerful practice. "Paying attention to the breath." It sounds so ordinary, doesn't it? But it's such a powerful method that if we're able to practice it often in everyday life, I think it will change our consciousness in a concrete, substantial way.

The point of this technique is not that we continuously have to pay attention to sensations in our body for a long a period of time. We can do it for a few seconds here and there in daily life to disrupt the momentum of the thinking mind that is propelled by unawareness, so that there is suddenly a space inside us where we can drop into rigpa.

Awareness of Space

Another method to be present is to be aware of the space in front of you or around you. Imagine you are working at your desk and get caught up in mental chatter related to your schedule or business with someone. Your whole being feels that you are dealing with something real. If you can just stop what you are doing, relax your eyes, and be aware of the space in front of you, without paying attention to any particular object, and feel that space, instantaneously everything stops.

When you allow yourself to be completely aware of pure space around you, you feel you are suddenly present, and then your mind is no longer lost in thoughts. All your problems and narratives are suddenly gone from the face of the earth. Then you can resume whatever you were doing from that spacious, empty mind, as if you turned a page in a notebook and now have an empty page.

Inquiry

There's a very powerful way to be fully present, which is taught in Dzogchen. It comes in the form of an inquiry. "Who is experiencing this?" This is also a very simple method. Let's say you are confused, are angry, or you are lost in sensory experiences. You can pause and ask, "Who is experiencing this?" And that question takes you back to yourself right there: to awareness—an undistracted, unbound, and egoless state—right away. It is a very effective way to disrupt the mind from falling into the mental traps of its experiences.

Six Consciousness Are Freed

Everything becomes quite simple when we discover that the root of suffering is the state of our mind when consciousness is lost in its experiences. How simple it is! Then the way to freedom is to be fully present and not lost in our experiences. That's the way to liberation. It's almost too simple.

Then there's a point where you don't even have to try to be present. Our habits of being lost in unawareness or in our experiences will go away eventually. Then you may have a new name: Tsokdruk Rangdrol. This is a very beautiful name that is often given to yogis. One of the most famous Dzogchen masters and author of *The Flight of Garuda* is also called Tsokdruk Rangdrol. The name Tsokdruk Rangdrol sounds very long and wordy when you translate it. But in Tibetan, it is a very beautiful name: "The natural liberation of the six fields of consciousness."

The idea is that you don't have to exert so much effort to try to awaken your consciousness. You don't even have to struggle to be present. You are living in awareness, a state of consciousness where you are free. Your consciousness is finally free from the grip of its ancient habit to get lost in its own experiences.

Then what do you do after that? That's a good question. If your mind becomes free—liberated from all these habits of being lost and abiding in nondual awareness, free from the shackle of suffering—what do you do? There's only one simple thing you do from then on: You celebrate existence. That's what you do.

An Invitation to Practice Every Moment

Can we use these methods more and more in our daily life so we can be present? While doing these practices, we will feel that we are present, in harmony with the way things are. The heart of the matter is to remember to be more and more present. This may be the only way we can really change our consciousness by shedding all the habits of unawareness.

Can we be more present with our breath as time goes by? Can we be present with our breath for a few seconds before we eat? Can we be fully present with the sensations in our feet when we get up, even for a few seconds? Or with the sensations in our body, here and there, in everyday life? Can we drop into awareness right away, in the here and now? Sometimes, no method is required. All you need is that one precious intention to stop perpetuating the thinking mind that is lost in itself. That one intention can immediately bring you back into awareness without any extra methods.

Can we be present with our body even in this very moment? Can we pause and ask, "Who is reading this book?" Isn't that an amazing inquiry? Ask that: "Who is reading this?"

Kyor Jung: Reviewing the Teachings

When you are confused, ask, "Who is confused?" When you are judging somebody, ask, "Who is judging?" In that moment, you are no longer lost in opinions. You are no longer lost in concepts. You are back to your true nature. You return to your home, your true home, where the true Padmasambhava resides—as the Fifth Dalai Lama said—in the center of our heart.

14

The Wish-Fulfilling Gem of Dzogchen

The Dzogchen teachings and practices are timeless, profound wisdom that allows us to find meaning, magic, purpose, and freedom in this very life. In some ways, we can regard the Dzogchen teachings as the *chintamani*, the wish-fulfilling gem mentioned in ancient Indian literature. Usually, one has to cross an ocean and go through a treacherous voyage to reach an island where such a gem may be found. Once you find it, you bring it home, and it has the power to grant all your wishes. But if you don't ask it for anything, it doesn't do anything for you.

In a similar way, the Dzogchen teachings are truly precious. They are the pinnacle of human wisdom. Yet without practicing them, we are like someone who possesses a wish-fulfilling gem but asks nothing of it, leaving our heart empty and our mind tormented.

We are living in an age of challenges brought about by external and internal factors. It seems there is more anxiety and neurosis on the rise. Maybe this situation is caused by the high speed of cultural changes brought by technology. But perhaps all these unsettling signs could be part of a giant evolution in consciousness that is happening rapidly, which may be the silver lining in this time as well.

Some tantras indicate that the general orthodox Buddhist practices may have corresponded to the spiritual needs of people who lived in the past, when life was much simpler and people were less complicated. Many of us have lived long enough to see the complex and unprecedented changes that have happened in the world.

I grew up in a very small village in Tibet. I remember that in general, even though people were not perfect, there was not so much neurosis or issues like anxiety, addiction, and mental problems. People were basically content with a simple way of life as long as they had their tea and tsampa (barley flour). There was no psychologist in my hometown. I don't think people even knew the word "psychology." There was a lot of joy. People could get together and drink tea all day, telling stories of their life. There was a general goodness, an unwritten rule that we should be kind and helpful to each other.

At that time, no one had a TV, but some families had a radio. Just like anywhere else, people needed entertainment, so people in my village often listened to traditional music on the radio. Another source of entertainment was to get together and invite someone who could read, since most elders in the village were illiterate. They would request that person to read great epics, such as *Gesar of Ling*, out loud.

No one was really wealthy; everyone had similar living standards, but at the same time, there was no sense of poverty. Fundamentally, there was a basic contentment in the community. There was not so much competition, comparison, or ambition, which is in striking juxtaposition to today's society.

Today, when I speak to people who grew up in my village, they say it has changed so much. It is completely modernized, and the younger generation is going through the same psychological and mental issues that are prevalent in many modern countries.

Take Refuge in Dzogchen

People today don't have the time to engage in some of the orthodox practices, such as being ordained as a monk, studying scriptures for years in the monastery, or practicing meditation in caves. People are also becoming more and more secular, and therefore they do not welcome the rigidity of some traditional dogma.

Because of their nature, Dzogchen teachings can be very helpful for people in today's world. Dzogchen is not dogmatic, and it is experiential as well as practical. It invites us to completely restructure our consciousness, turning it inside out.

Many of us know that the problems in our lives cannot be solved until we figure out how to fundamentally shake up the structure of our consciousness. We need a serious internal overhaul. This is true both for individuals and society in general. As long as we don't bring about a profound shift in our consciousness, no matter what we do in order to find happiness and peace, or solutions to our problems, we won't achieve what we want.

Most problems come from the state of consciousness that we live in, and the solution comes from consciousness as well. But as a famous saying goes, "Solutions can never come from the same state of mind that created the problem in the first place." I think this is totally right. This is an age-old human predicament, a blunder that we keep repeating. We are always trying to solve problems with the same state of mind that created them.

This does not mean we should sit back and do nothing, and let all the wrongs in society and our own lives continue. But at the end of the day, we have to come back to ourselves, go inside, and realize that if we don't restructure the foundation of consciousness, there may not be authentic positive changes. Wangari Maathai, an environmentalist from Kenya and the first black African woman to win the Nobel Peace Prize, said,

> There comes a time when humanity is called to shift to a new level of consciousness, to reach a higher moral ground. A time when we have to shed our fear and give hope to each other. That time is now.[†]

To me, the Dzogchen teachings are so powerful that they can completely transform our consciousness if we understand and apply them. Dzogchen teachings are not another set of Buddhist practices or philosophy. They immediately turn us inward and invite us to experience a state of consciousness that is already enlightened and free from the grip of ego and all our other neuroses. We can go beyond our limited concepts, theories, ideas, and thoughts to see the liberating nature of reality as it is. This also allows us to tap into the innate, inexhaustible spiritual resources of love and joy that lie within each of us.

[†] Wangari Maathai. Nobel Lecture. Nobel Peace Prize, December 10, 2004. Oslo, Norway. Accessed July 26, 2025. https://www.nobelprize.org/prizes/peace/2004/maathai/lecture/

The Wish-Fulfilling Gem of Dzogchen

The True Hidden Kingdom

Those who come to Dzogchen teachings or have an interest in them must have some openness in their minds to experience the freedom and liberation that comes from awakening to the nature of mind, which is the heart of Dzogchen. Our interest in Dzogchen is our deepest desire to experience transcendence. Such a desire should be cultivated. Even though it is intrinsic to us, sometimes that desire is not awake, especially when we get stuck in our ego or lost in the worldly affairs of each day.

Many traditions in the East developed methodologies designed to help us cultivate such a desire, which is called the "longing for liberation." Sometimes this desire kicks in naturally; other times, it arises when our suffering reaches such a level that it is painful even to exist, and we are forced to seek the ultimate liberation.

In Tibetan culture, there is the concept of a sacred place that is hidden and cannot be easily reached by people, where you can leave all problems behind—personal, political, and everything that drives you crazy. These places, which are considered magical and enchanted, are called *beyul*. Many Tibetan Buddhist teachers in the Nyingma tradition, such as Longchenpa, often longed to travel to those places when they felt the world around them was descending into darkness.

Longchenpa wrote an entire hymn about going away from the world and entering the beyul. In that poem, he said the time to go there is when the world and people around us are changing too fast, filled with fighting and conflict. When he said "changing," he meant not in a good way. He also referred to the time when ruthless invaders were about to come. During the period of history when he lived, the fourteenth century, Tibet was not completely peaceful due to political turbulence. Many Buddhist teachers at that time felt that certain frontier regions in southern Tibet were the beyul, the perfect ideal place, which were not so influenced by what was going on in the rest of Tibet.

Today, we live in a very different time, but every now and then, we may have a desire to go somewhere else when we feel that our society is descending or filled with too much turmoil. Or we may imagine a more desirable life when we are unhappy with our own life.

But the truth is that the beyul is in each of us. It is the state of our own mind. Rigpa is the true beyul. Through Dzogchen practice and teachings, we can open the door to that hidden kingdom inside. There is no need to wait to find it, and no need to go anywhere. *Now* is always the time to enter it. Once we enter it, we are able to travel on the amazing journey called human life with much more meaning and joy.

Appendix
Guided Meditation

A guided meditation is provided below. Readers may choose to practice by following the written instructions, or, for their convenience, access a recorded version at www.shambhala.com/releasingtheknotofthemind/meditations. Whenever you are ready to meditate formally, the first step is to pick the space where you are going to meditate. It doesn't matter if it is in a temple, home, or outdoors. Traditionally, most people meditate on a cushion, but it is fine to sit on a chair if that works for you.

Shamatha

Take a few moments to give rise to bodhichitta, the awakened heart, our highest aspiration, our commitment to walk this path of love and wisdom in order to be fully awakened for the benefit of all beings without any exclusion. Feel that now your heart is filled with the blessings of the bodhicitta.

Appendix

As a reminder, you might like to settle into your body energetically. Allow yourself to feel that you are here. You are fully present here. Being aware of our body is a wonderful doorway to the present moment. Just feel your attention is no longer scattered, and you are here completely. Notice there is a sense of being grounded and centered simply from returning to the body from the virtual reality of mind-manufactured stories and opinions.

Then you might like to have your back straight. Let your shoulders relax. You can rest your hands on your knees or join them. Feel that now you are grounded in your body with dignity, but also with a sense of ease and in the state of equilibrium. Feel that your energy is flowing with ease.

Feel you are sitting in a posture that is comfortable, that allows you to feel stillness that comes naturally. Feel that you are in a perfect state of being for meditation.

Now just drop into your body. Notice the physical sensations—sensations in your feet, in your belly, in your chest. Embrace those sensations as a doorway to be in the present moment. Notice that the moment you drop into your body, your mind is no longer wandering in the virtual reality of the past and the future, but you are completely here. Notice there's a quality of benevolence, of being fully here.

You might like to close your eyes. Then bring your attention to your breath. Let go of your thoughts and continuously pay attention to each breath for a while—each in-breath and each out-breath. Especially notice the breath in your nostrils.

As you notice each breath, you might want to become aware of the subtle sensations and changes that accompany the pathway of each breath. Notice that when you breathe in, the temperature in your nostrils is slightly cooler, and when you breathe out, it gets a little warmer. When you breathe in, your shoulders rise slightly.

Without putting too much effort, make sure that you are present with each breath. If you become aware of these subtleties, this helps you not get distracted by thoughts and stay in concentration. It helps you stay interested in the process of breathing. The more interested you are in breathing, the more you can be present with concentration.

If a thought arises, don't follow it. Remember to come back to the breath immediately. Then our coarse, active thoughts subside. There's only stillness and silence. Cherish this inner silence that unfolds right away the moment you bring your attention to your breath. Enjoy that silence as if you are drinking the nectar of tranquility.

Open Awareness

Now let go of your concentration on the breath. Then just rest in the natural state of your mind. Don't try to meditate. Don't try to concentrate. Just be. Notice that now there is just awareness—awareness that is aware of all these things that are happening on their own as an expression of life or nature. Feel free to open your eyes, or you can close them whenever you want.

APPENDIX

Notice that you are now abiding in the mode of nondoing. You are not trying to make anything happen, yet sights, sounds, sensations, and moods are all unfolding as life channels through you. Then relax into such an open and spacious awareness. Let it just unfold.

When you let go of a single-pointed concentration, be curious about what thoughts might arise. Thoughts will begin to arise. You don't have to do anything to produce them. Thoughts are a part of nature. But here we have the choice not to identify with our thoughts. Whereas in our everyday life, we are always following our thoughts. But here, thoughts are just a part of nature. You can just regard them as the display of the ineffable or the dharmakaya mind. They are not even yours.

Notice that there is a profound freedom when you experience that thoughts are no longer yours. Notice the difference between the state of your mind right now versus your state of mind in everyday life. Notice that in the present moment, thoughts are arising, but you are no longer thinking.

Let all the thoughts arise. It doesn't matter where they are coming from or what is causing them. Don't own them. Treat them as if they are not yours anymore, as an impersonal phenomenon, like a cloud drifting or rain falling or waves on the ocean. Remember that when you watch waves on the ocean, you don't identify with them.

Guided Meditation

Continuously relax in open awareness. Stay openhearted with whatever life is presenting to you. Sound. Sensations. Thoughts. This is open awareness or vipashyana, or you can call this rigpa in the Dzogchen language.

Longchenpa said the perfect place to practice open awareness is on the top of a mountain, where you have a panoramic view. But what he meant is to just open the windows of your senses and allow yourself to enjoy witnessing sound, sight, touch, taste, and smell. Welcome everything. Sensations. Moods. Boredom. Joy. Stillness. Comfort. Being at ease. Pleasant sensations or unpleasant ones. Thoughts—whether positive or unwholesome. Welcome all of them without any preference.

Then remember not to follow your thoughts. Don't judge whatever rises in your awareness.

Now and then, pause and see what is happening in your mind. You can ask, "Am I fully present or am I lost in my thoughts?" Then let go of the inquiry. Come back to awareness. You might like to do this inquiry every now and then.

Relax into awareness and notice how alive, vibrant, and rich reality is—colors, thoughts, sensations are constantly dissolving and arising. Allow yourself to be aware of this dynamic, ever-changing nature of existence, life, or reality.

Appendix

Open awareness is not about going into any particular state of mind but being fully present and being with everything while letting go of preference.

Enjoy what this show called "life" is manifesting by itself—thoughts, sensations, colors, sounds. You are no longer the doer. You are no longer trying to make anything happen. You are no longer struggling. You are simply witnessing. You are awareness. There is no separation between you and awareness. You are free, uncontracted, spacious, and openhearted.

Stay in that awareness as long as you want. Whenever you are ready to end the meditation, you might like to take a few moments to vow to yourself that you will incorporate this experience into the rest of your day.

About the Author

Anam Thubten grew up in Tibet and at an early age began to practice in the Nyingma tradition of Tibetan Buddhism. He is the founder and spiritual advisor of Dharmata Foundation and Kailash Fellowship. One of his main projects is preserving the lineage of Dudjom Lingpa in the modern world. Anam Thubten teaches widely in the United States and abroad. More information about Anam Thubten, including his teaching calendar, can be found online at dharmata.org. Anam Thubten's published books in English include the following:

Voice of the Primordial Buddha: A Commentary on the Sharp Vajra of Awareness by Dudjom Lingpa

Citadel of Awareness: A Commentary on Jigme Lingpa's Dzogchen Aspiration Prayer

Fragrance of Emptiness: A Commentary on the Heart Sutra

Into the Haunted Ground: A Guide to Cutting the Root of Suffering

About the Author

A Sacred Compass: Navigating Life Through the Bardo Teachings

Choosing Compassion: How to Be of Benefit in a World That Needs Our Love

No Self, No Problem

Several of these books have also been translated into various languages. In addition, Anam Thubten has authored several books and many articles in Tibetan.